Restful Anticipation

Finding contentment in seasons of waiting

Melissa Miller

Copyright © 2020 by Melissa Miller
ISBN: 978-1-7358538-1-9

Copyright © 2020 by Melissa Miller

Editor: Maddie Buck

All Rights Reserved.

Printed in the United States of America

Scripture quotations labeled ESV are from The Holy Bible, English Standard Version®). Copyright © 2001 by Crossway, a publishing ministry of Good News Publishers. Used by permission. All right reserved. ESV® Text Edition: 2016

Scripture quotations marked MSG are taken from THE MESSAGE, copyright © 1993, 2002, 2018 by Eugene H. Peterson. Used by permission of NavPress. All rights reserved. Represented by Tyndale House Publishers, Inc.

Scripture quotations marked HCSB are taken from the Holman Christian Standard Bible®, Copyright © 1999, 2000, 2002, 2003, 2009 by Holman Bible Publishers. Used by permission. Holman Christian Standard Bible®, Holman CSB®, and HCSB® are federally registered trademarks of Holman Bible Publishers.

Scripture quotations marked TPT are from The Passion Translation®. Copyright © 2017, 2018 by Passion & Fire Ministries, Inc. Used by permission. All rights reserved. ThePassionTranslation.com.

Scripture quotations marked NLT are taken from the *Holy Bible*, New Living Translation, copyright © 1996, 2004, 2015 by Tyndale House Foundation. Used by permission of Tyndale House Publishers, Inc., Carol Stream, Illinois 60188. All rights reserved.

PRAISE FOR

Restful Anticipation:
Finding Contentment in Seasons of Waiting

"Whether you're waiting to find your husband, struggling with infertility, waiting for test results, or the fulfillment of a dream, this book will refresh your soul!

In her book *Restful Anticipation,* Melissa captures God's heart to provide encouragement during prolonged seasons of waiting. Within the following pages you'll discover inspiring stories, powerful truths, and experience a renewed strength to persevere. Most of all, Melissa's writing will masterfully lead you to the arms of *The One* who holds your future."

Julie Gorman
Founder of Restore Family & Married for a Purpose, Author of *What I Wish My Mother Told Me About Men*, *What I Wish My Mother Told Me About Marriage, Gentle Whispers* and *Married for a Purpose.*

Contents

Introduction 1

Chapter 1: Hope Deferred 7

Chapter 2: Edges of Trust 31

Chapter 3: Contentment 43

Chapter 4: Wrestle Through the Wait 61

Chapter 5: Weary in the Wait 85

Chapter 6: Staying Power 103

Chapter 7: Almosts 119

Chapter 8: Holding Places 135

Chapter 9: Expectations 151

Chapter 10: Unresolved Endings 165

Epilogue 178

Acknowledgements 180

Endnotes 18

Introduction

Someone once said to me, "If you pray for patience, God will give you something to be patient about." It made God seem like a stern father driving an Oldsmobile station wagon, warning us kids in the back, "Stop crying, or I'll give you something to cry about!"

When anxiousness rises within me, I know I lack patience, but I find myself tiptoeing around my request.

Lord, I pray for pat— (wait, will He give me more to be patient for if I pray for this?) I pray for...grace. Yes, your grace, I need more of your grace for this situation in my life, Lord. Amen.

Our adoption journey began over five years ago. I never expected to wait this long for a match. My biological kids sprout up like bamboo shoots;

only one of them still fits comfortably in my lap and takes the occasional piggyback ride. But I'm not done with piggyback rides and story time. I'm not done with plastic horses lined up across the ledge of my bathtub and stuffed animals squeezed between the posts in our staircase banister. A child grows, not in my belly, but in my heart. I'm ready ... but I'm still waiting.

Brandon, my husband, was adopted at birth. I was unofficially adopted as a teenager. Adoption, for us, seems as normal as our names. It's always been there, woven into our stories and our identities. When people ask Brandon if he knew he was adopted, he jokes, "I knew. I thought everyone was adopted. Isn't that how babies work?"

I've come to view waiting like a detour. I used to think the only people who enjoy detours are the twenty-somethings on college break, looking for a spontaneous adventure and a good story to tell. Then I met my husband, the man who *lives* for detours. Every start of the engine marks an invitation for a new adventure. Brandon seeks out the longer route for the sake of exploring. Most of the time, it drives me nuts, but I'll admit, it pays off sometimes.

"Would you mind if we took a different route?" Brandon asks (while adjusting the GPS to an off-beaten path). In those moments, I want to pound my head against the glass and yell, "Why?! Don't you understand efficiency?" Instead, I take a deep breath and reluctantly give the go-ahead. (I later discovered Brandon sneakily plots some detours without me knowing.) Mostly, I'm convinced it's all a waste of time. But now and then, Brandon's rerouting takes my breath away. Don't tell him this, but some of our favorite spots come from his ridiculous detours. A few years ago, during one of my husband's rerouting whims, we found a dreamy open house that became home. Brandon is the perfect match for me, always helping me find beauty in the slower path.

I fight against this lesson stubbornly, but I've come to believe I can view detours one of two ways. I can view them as a giant orange roadblock sign, locking me in a traffic jam, or like a winding back road with captivating scenic views. When God leads me down the slow path, I'm learning to focus on the beauty rather than the delay.

Driving back from South Carolina one night, we experienced this. Typically, we like to make the drive as short as possible. It's exactly 7.5 hours from our house in Florida to Grammy's house in Aiken without any stops. We pee quickly, we eat quickly, and we fill the car up quickly. We want to watch a few movies and make it there. Same drill on the way back. One night, the road faded dark, and we couldn't see a thing on either side of us. Our headlights only illuminated a short path ahead; Brandon eased on the gas pedal halfway expecting something to jump out at us. One of the kids pushed the button above them. We offer the reminder there is no point in opening the moonroof when it's dark - there's nothing to see. Before the skylight opens fully, we all gasp in unison. The stars were unlike anything we'd ever seen before, brilliant and copious. The stars dazzled the sky with radiance, winking at us. Like a crowd chanting our names, we couldn't resist their stunning invitation.

"Pull the car over." I smack Brandon's arm.

"Ouch! Okay, okay!" Brandon says as he slows the car down and pulls over to the right-hand side of the road. We all roll down our windows, and the kids pop their heads out of the top of the skylight. As my window rolls down, I gasp again. We've mostly lived in bigger cities; the stars on the backcountry roads of South Carolina were unlike anything we'd ever seen. I hear the hum of the crickets and the buzz of the cicadas. I feel the warm air on my face, and I see nothing but glitter in the sky.

"It's magical," I say. "It's just magical."
Brandon asks if I want to get out of the car, and I say no. I've grown to embrace detours a little more, but

not enough to face mosquitos in the South.

That dreamy night is a slice of where I'm heading; God showing me the beauty in the slower route, showing me the gift in the wait. Jesus teaches me how to trust Him, reminding me of His sovereignty over what I see as a delay.

This book is about finding contentment in your season of waiting. Over the past five years, we've gone through many ups and downs waiting to adopt. The long journey tested our faith in unimaginable ways. At times our path felt more like a mechanical breakdown than a scenic route. Our adoption almost fell through altogether. We moved across the country, and let's say the cross-country road trip taught us a lot about waiting. We now refer to that trip as a favorite family memory that we'd never want to repeat.

Whether your season of waiting feels more like a breakdown, a scenic route, or an adventure that you'd never want to repeat, I've been there. I know what it feels like to be completely confused during the detours. I know what it's like to not feel like yourself for a season. I know how it feels to wonder about your sense of purpose and ask God if He's punishing you or putting you on a shelf. And after tirelessly waiting, praying, and financially investing, I know what it's like to lay every option on the table and surrender to the possibility of a new ending to your story. Most importantly, I know how to cross over from restless to restful. Something shifted in me. I'm going to try my best to multiply what God did in my heart and deposit it into yours. Let's go on a journey to a place I call *Restful Anticipation.*

Chapter One: Hope Deferred

Peanut butter jars. That's my waiting nemesis; stirring peanut butter jars. Everyone knows it's essential to mix the top layer of oil into the peanut butter at the right pace. Otherwise, you risk getting the outside of the jar all sticky and wasting the precious commodity of peanut butter. I typically leave the peanut-butter-stirring job to my husband, but when he's out of town, I'm out of options. I stare down the peanut butter jar like I'm in a western showdown.

I take a firm stance. I grip the jar tighter than Thor grips his hammer. I wield the perfect stirring spoon. I smugly look down at the pitiful pot while stirring at a steady pace. It doesn't stand a chance. But before my smugness turns into gloating, my phone dings or one of my kids' yells, "MOM!" The peanut butter takes advantage of my distracted and impatient state and begins crawling out, sneaking its way down the sides of the jar. PB planned this all along. Due to my diverted attention, my once steady stirring pace quickens, and the peanut butter is now The Blob, alive and infiltrating my kitchen counters with its sticky presence. I spend more time cleaning up the jar and the counter than I did stirring; impatience never pays off.

When I first met my husband in college, his patience stood out to me. His ability to listen endlessly to someone's problems is nothing short of a superpower. He listens without an agenda; he empathizes and encourages. He takes things in stride. He makes everyone feel like the most important person in the room. Despite watching him cruise around campus on a longboard in sweatpants, I still went up to my dorm room and told my roommate, "Whoever marries Brandon Miller will be the luckiest girl in the world."

Well, as luck would have it, Brandon liked my get-er-done personality, proof that opposites attract. Over seventeen years later, Brandon still remains patient with my task-focused tendencies. I observe him gracefully shift from work-mode to husband-mode to dad-mode and then back to work mode. I tilt my head like a confused robot, watching this foreign ability. Must. Learn. This. Skill. I thrive on efficiency; the very word lights me up. I want to see every box checked, and I'll go to great lengths to figure out a way to do it faster the next time. How can one stop in the middle of a task to happily talk to people? I don't get it.

Don't get me wrong. I love people, but I hit a limit, and I need alone time to recharge. As you can imagine, my drive for efficiency creates unrest. Brandon (and Jesus) show me how to be more fully present, enjoy the moment, and slow down. I'm a stubbornly slow learner, though, sometimes in denial of my own pace. When I'm focused on a task, I don't like to take a break to pee or eat. I wish I were kidding. I'd probably stop breathing if I thought it'd save me time. But over the last sixteen years of marriage, my favorite memories were not when I'm in my pee-holding, hangry, work-mode. My favorite memories include spontaneously swimming in our skivvies at the Hobe Sound beach, getting snowed in at a cabin in Big Bear, or the peaceful tick-tock of the baby swing holding my newborns.

I'm at my best when I take life in stride like Brandon, allowing room for spontaneity, delays, and slowing down. But too often, I find myself slipping back into old habits. I throw something in a drawer because I lack the patience to put it in its proper place. I skip a step in the recipe and end up ruining the dish. I rush through shaving my legs and need band-aids for my shins. I grab a snack to hold me over instead of making a proper lunch.

I don't have to look far to find people who share my same struggle. Others might keep their peanut butter jars squeaky clean, but they anxiously inch forward every three seconds at stoplights. We all have our own waiting pet-peeves, waiting in line at the grocery store, elevators, commercial breaks, internet connection, or waiting for the child to finish their story about Minecraft. Culture only reinforces the "your way, right away" mentality. You can find an instant version of almost anything nowadays: instant coffee, instant mac n' cheese, instant mashed potatoes, instant rice, instant oatmeal; you name it. And if you can't find it in instant form, don't worry, you can cook it in your Instant Pot.

We've all heard the infamous 1 Corinthians 13 verse about love. We hear the scripture at weddings, at funerals, at church, and in Hallmark cards. We love talking about love, don't we? People use the Corinthians passage as the quintessential definition of love, so naturally, we like to refer back to it. What's funny is that no one pays much attention to the first line in verse four: love is patient. In a list of what love is, the scriptures name patience first. We don't hear about it much, because it's not glamorous. Patience is the stock ingredient in the recipe for love.

It's not the spicy dash at the end or the exciting, unique twist, but it's the essential base. God teaching us patience doesn't sound very exciting, but without it, we don't have real love.

In the last several years, I've read countless books on rest, slowing down, or soul-care in hopes of growing more patience as we wait for our child. In the adoption world, they call it "paper pregnant." Our child grows in our hearts instead of our tummies. We experience nesting, just like a normal pregnancy. We also experience a yearning to meet our child, a deep desire to see their face and know their name. At least a few times a month, I get the feeling someone is missing from our family. I tally every head; we're all accounted for. I remind myself we only have five members in our family for now. I can't help feeling the incompleteness of my family. It's like one of my children is at a sleepover, and I keep forgetting to pick them up. It's similar to the feeling I get when my kids burrow in the store's clothing racks. *Where are they hiding?*

The Stocking

My heart for adoption began in my teenage years, growing slowly over time. At age fourteen, my peers at school asked me, "Why do you live at Brittany's house?" I hated that question; I hated feeling different. And frankly, I wasn't sure how to respond to why I moved in with my best friend's family. Do I tell them the blunt truth, that my mom hit me with a car while she was high, so CPS got involved? It seemed a little TMI (Too Much Information). Like a seasoned politician, I found ways to respond without actually answering the question. But no packaged response sums up a complicated family history. It doesn't tell the full story of how, despite my mom's addiction, she still circled all the "A's" on my report cards and hung them on her fridge, stroked my forehead every time I was sick as a child, and believed that I could be the world's greatest anything. My mom tragically died when I was sixteen years old, so I keep those good memories alive and hold them close. I'm not excusing her behavior, but I found freedom the day I decided not to make her the villain of my story.

The day my mom hit me with the car was brutal. We had a huge fight, and something about the emptiness of my mom's eyes terrified me. When she was on drugs, it was only the shell of my mother. It's surreal feeling homesick for someone standing right in front of you. I made a swift decision, not knowing it would impact the rest of my life; I ran away.

Brittany's mom, Jenna, took me under her wing and into their home. Technically, I became a foster teen, but I never felt like one. They welcomed me into every aspect of their lives; meals, sports, family functions, and even holidays. The first Christmas I spent there, I felt shocked to see my name on a stocking hanging on the mantle. I did a double take. I did not deserve that place, but my name lined up with all the biological children. It will pass, I convinced myself. *They will see my faults and grow sick of me, and by next year the stocking won't be up.*

Nearly 25 years later, I still have a Christmas stocking hanging with my name on it, except now it says, "The Millers" and includes my husband and children. Next to my stocking hangs my little sister's, since Jenna eventually took her in too. It wasn't a legal adoption but remains official in all our hearts. Jenna became "Mom" to my sister and me and "Nanny" to our kids (she's originally from England and makes sure to tell us often she loves us "oodles and gobs"). Most of the time, I call her Nanny (it makes me feel cultured or something).

One well-meaning person corrected my language, suggesting I use the term 'kinship care' to describe my adoption since it wasn't official, and I knew the family beforehand. I asked Nanny what she thought of that, and she sent me a five-page text full of crying and angry emojis. Here is a small preview:

"Maybe that person thinks an official adoption would have made your life different. It wouldn't have. You are you. I am me. My heart loves you. I still would have made the same mistakes. I would still have loved every single day, moment, and second. I still would have been there while you cheered or did math that I didn't understand at the kitchen table. I would have still cried in the bathroom when your purse got stolen at school, and you cried because they poked the eyes out of your ID card—or been proud of you as a cheerleader. I'd still go there when you had Mother/Daughter day/week at college. I'd still be there when you got married. I still would have gotten a wedding cake that wasn't the right kind, and it still would have melted. I'd still make sure I was there when the kids were born; I'd still cry, laugh, bake, and make chicken soup. I'd still do all those things even if there were a "legal" adoption. But I don't need that. My heart adopted you. That's more important and more binding to me than a piece of paper ever could be."

So, I won't be referring to my adoption as kinship care because no one likes making their momma cry. And for those of us with a not-so-normal childhood, we've had to find our sense of family through more than blood and paperwork.

I do understand the raw spots of adoptees, though. Even my husband, who has a "fairy tale" adoption story, eventually encountered his own trauma. The story of how he discovered his birth family is one for the books, and at the same time, it surfaced in him a cocktail of unexpected emotions. Every adoptee, birth family, and adoptive family must find their own norms, own language, and own unique titles. An instruction manual doesn't exist for the not-so-normal family.

At my wedding, a second set of bridesmaids stood with me at the altar – all women (including Nanny) who stepped in as mother-figures in the wake of my mom's death. I shared vows with a man adopted at birth. My dad walked me down the aisle, never telling a soul that I wasn't biologically his. Brandon and I shared communion at the altar, giving thanks to a Father in Heaven who adopted me into His family and kingdom. I didn't know what our future had in store, only that I longed to hang a stocking up for a child the way someone did for me.

Still Waiting

When we started the adoption process, we patted ourselves on the back for completing a big stack of papers. *Whoa, people weren't kidding; that was a lot of work*, we thought. It took about a month to get everything together, and we went out to dinner to celebrate our accomplishments as if we passed a rigorous college exam. We later discovered we had only completed the preliminary application. We already felt paper-weary, and we'd only scratched the surface. We unwittingly celebrated far too early.

After the preliminary application came the home study paperwork. We went through psychological evaluations, adoption training and conferences, family information, CPR and first aid training, home inspections, fingerprints, pool safety courses, background checks, interviews, and much more. (We completed much of the process over again with each yearly renewal.) I'm not complaining; I'm thankful for reputable agencies and the Hague Convention ensuring adoptions are above-board. It's vital to vet adoptive families properly; it just doesn't make the process easy to go through.

The adoption halts if we neglect to turn in one piece of paperwork, fail one test, miss a deadline, or grow weary and don't follow through. I remind myself that swimming in this sea of paperwork will be worth it. I envision holding my child in my arms for the first time, telling them how they've grown in our hearts over the years. I picture our kids playing tag with their new brother or sister and showing them how to play our favorite family games.

Buzzing with excitement, our kids hung "we are adopting!" notes on the fridge in their little jagged handwriting. Sticky notes with crayon drawings about our adoption decorated our coffee table and the bathroom mirror. When pregnant with my youngest, the older children rubbed my belly, speaking softly to their new sibling. "I can't wait to meet you. I can't wait to play with you." I sensed the post-it notes and drawings were my kids' way of rubbing my belly and saying the same thing; *I can't wait to meet you, I can't wait to play with you.*

We shopped for cribs, car seats, outlet plugs, mattress protectors, and safety locks, just in case. I even found the perfect books to read to my future child to help them understand both the beauty and loss of adoption.

Our agency gave us an 18-24 month wait time. We began our countdown the day we submitted the preliminary application. Once that eighteen-month marked rolled around, my excitement felt palpable. "Any day now!" I'd smile at Brandon, keeping my ringer on loud as we awaited the phone call that would change our lives.

The months rolled on and on, and eventually, we touched base with our agency. "Any day now, right?" we asked.

"Well, it's typically 18-24 months from the time the country receives and approves your dossier." They responded.

I felt stupid. I counted the months from our preliminary application, which was merely the application to work with our agency. Of course, the wait countdown begins after the country receives and approves our dossier. I amped up my family sky-high with anticipation of our child's arrival, and our wait was just beginning. Our photographer friend took gorgeous photos of our family announcing our adoption after we submitted the preliminary application. I held colorful balloons in my hand, and the kids each held up a sign; one said "we," the next said "are," and the final sign said "ADOPTING!" As excited as we were, that premature announcement only led to a series of questions from friends and family.

"So, what's going on with the adoption? Any news?"

"Still waiting!"

We probably should have just put a sign on our door that said, "Still waiting."

After starting at ground zero in our wait time, we decided not to think about it as much. But our kids, especially our son, asked about it regularly. "How much longer? It's taking so long!" Night after night, when we'd tuck him in for bed, he'd ask us to pray for his little brother, wherever he was out there. He asked Jesus to help the process to go faster, and then he'd ask us why his prayers weren't working. We told our son about the paperwork and God's timing, but his head still dropped with disappointment. Our hearts sunk alongside his.

Have you ever felt like you were made for something you've never done before? A friend of mine felt called to be a mom all her life. It was the only thing in her life she felt certain of. As a little girl, she played dolls, dressing her future children up, spoon-feeding them applesauce. As an adult, she feels perpetually confused and heartbroken when she faces another negative pregnancy test every month.

I can't imagine the heartbreak of infertility, and in no way does our wait compare, but I can relate to our dear friend's deferred hope. At first, we felt full of faith that our child or children were right around the corner, but with each passing month and year, our faith faded into a dull ache. Have you ever experienced this ache of deferred hope? Proverbs 13:12 (ESV) says, "Hope deferred makes the heart sick."

Here's the good news: A sick heart isn't a dead heart. It isn't even a terminally ill heart. It's just weak. It's tired. It needs some bone broth and a good rest. It raced around the track hard and fast, and now it's time for a pit stop. I'm coming to believe God uses these pit stops for a purpose. Pit stops ensure drivers can finish the race. But in our minds, we hold timelines and deadlines, presupposing an arrival at a certain destination within a certain time frame. We always feel we should be further along than we are, caught up running a race against our expectations. A.W. Tozer's quote is a great reminder that our timelines don't match God's:

"God never hurries. There are no deadlines against which he must work. Only to know this is to quiet our spirits and relax our nerves."[i]

Purpose in the Postponement

In John 11 (HCSB), Mary and Martha sent word to Jesus that their brother Lazarus was sick, they said, "Lord, the one you love is sick." Jesus seems to contradict himself in his response to Mary and Martha. At first, He says Lazarus' sickness will not end in death, and later He tells them Lazarus is dead and He's glad He wasn't there for their sake. *Huh?* I can only imagine their pain, confusion, and angst. By the time Jesus finally arrives (after deliberately prolonging the journey), Lazarus was dead, gone, stinky, and in the tomb for four days. It's important to note that Jesus didn't delay because He had some prior speaking engagement or appointment at the temple.

A prolonged waiting season will test our faith in unimaginable ways. Do we believe that God is good? Where is God when one of the deepest desires of our heart appears breathless and lifeless? How can we trust a God who causes intentional and heartbreaking delays?

When Mary later sees Jesus, she speaks the same words as Martha, "Lord, if only you had been here, my brother would not have died."

If I had a quarter for all my "If Onlys."

If only God intervened.

If only God opened that one door.

If only God moved a little faster.

If only God answered the prayer sooner.

If only, and maybe our hope wouldn't be deferred, and our heart wouldn't be sick, right? *If only.*

The days drudged on like decades for the sisters waiting for Jesus to save their brother. With each passing minute, the light of hope dims as his body decays. With every shift in the fading sun, Mary and Martha must wonder, *what could be more important than this?* Jesus sees Mary's tears and responds to her *if only*. What does He have to say for Himself? What explanation does He provide for His unacceptable tardiness? What could Jesus possibly offer at this point?

In verse 35, John records one of the most profound moments in scripture:

Jesus wept.

These words, these two little words, bid me to drop my guard and set down my sword. These words inch toward me, inviting me to inch toward them.

Jesus wept.

The tender words form into vines, growing around my calloused heart, softening me. When I expect a gavel, Jesus brings a tear. His tears puzzle and pause me, and I'm betting the sisters didn't know what to make of Jesus' tears either.

Jesus sees the sisters' tears, and He feels their pain. He is greatly troubled and deeply moved in His spirit. But Jesus didn't rush to the solution; He didn't skip over or dismiss the emotion. Jesus validates the pain and the disappointment, and (spoiler alert) even though He knows He will raise Lazarus from the dead, what does He do? He weeps.

Why didn't Jesus get there sooner? Why did Jesus cause the delay? And if Jesus knows He's going to raise Lazarus from the dead, why allow the pain and sadness beforehand? I don't know. But we see sides of Jesus in this story that show us His character. We see Him drawing near to the brokenhearted, weeping with them in their pain. We see Jesus, without hesitation, approaching the dead, decaying, and foul odored. We see Jesus praying to the Father. We see Jesus as a miracle-worker, bringing death to life, turning around an impossible situation. I don't know the purpose of the postponement, but I am thankful that John took the time to record the story, especially those two little words.

Pastor Ryan McDermott shared a story once

about the beautiful birds in his backyard that kept running into his window. Every few months, Ryan buried another bird who fell victim at his window, which hurt his heart every time. One day, one of the birds survived. It took a beating, but it had a chance. He tried scooping up the injured little bird, but in fear, it kept flitting away. He followed the bird while it fluttered like a grasshopper through the yard. *If only I were a bird, then I could speak bird*, the man thought. *If I became a bird and could speak bird, then the bird would know that I'm not here to hurt it; I'm here to help. If only I could speak bird, I could tell the bird that I'm not here to bring harm; I'm here to rescue it.* As soon as Ryan finished his thought, he remembered the gospel.

God found a way, didn't he? God found a way to become human so that he could speak human. His son Jesus is a miracle and a miracle-worker, but instead of domineering us with His divinity, He stoops down to weep with us in our humanity. This is what disarms me, that Christ does not stand as a distant spectator to my disappointment and my pain. He climbs inside, bringing compassion and comfort, empathy and assurance. His tears remind me that He's here to help and not to harm. His spirit was there when, as a teenager, I fell into a pile of laundry, sobbing at the news of my mother's death; and it's here with me now, in the disappointment of our adoption story. He's present in life's jarring stabs but also there in the dull aches.

Psalm 34:18 soothes my soul:

"The Lord is near the broken-hearted, He saves those crushed in spirit."

The Message translation says it this way, *"If your heart is broken, you'll find God right there; if you're kicked in the gut, He'll help you catch your breath."*

When our heart feels broken, and our hope is deferred, God is near. He isn't far off, in the clouds, elusive, or playing hide-and-seek. He's right there. So very close. And when we feel like our heart is dead, even death isn't final in God's kingdom.

It's okay to acknowledge the disappointment. While we aim to follow truth instead of feelings, it doesn't mean our feelings don't journey with us; they just don't always get the driver's seat. Jesus doesn't want us to fake it until we make it. He wants a real relationship, where we never hesitate to meet Him right where we are. Often, we want to meet Jesus where we think we should be - or where we wish we were. We muster up a pretty prayer, package it with a bow, and wonder why our prayers feel flat. God already knows exactly where we are and what's in our hearts. He knows the thoughts we think before we think them. There's no point in hiding. But, like Adam and Eve, we cover ourselves, resist vulnerability, and fear drawing near to God. As we remember Jesus' divinity, we can't forget His humanity. *Jesus wept.* He's not here to harm; He's here to help.

When you arrive at a shopping mall, one of the first things you do is look at the directory. The tall display maps out the shops, and you scan for the yellow star labeled "you are here." Determining your starting point is critical before you can take the first step toward your endpoint. Without this knowledge, you'll wander aimlessly, hoping to end up in your desired destination eventually.

Let's be honest about where we are. Where is your little yellow star on the map? How far away is it from where you want to be? We all need a moment to process, and in time, we need to move forward. We can't stay stagnant either. I've found great value in both processing and in moving forward. We'll move forward soon, but let's not rush through this critical phase of accepting our little yellow star, even though it's not where we want it to be. After all, allowing our hearts to run ahead of God's timing instead of resting in it is what made our hearts sick in the first place. Let's hand over our *if onlys* and let the expert heart-mender draw near.

A Prayer for The Hope-Deferred

Father, thank you for your presence. Thank you that you are near to the broken-hearted. Thank you that you have a plan in my delay and in my season of waiting. Thank you that you don't dismiss me, my feelings, or my pain. You weep with me. Thank you that even though I don't know how my situation will work out, you do. Thank you that you are always with me every step of the way. Thank you that I can rest in that truth today - the truth of your nearness and your compassion. Thank you that you will never leave me and never forsake me. I pray that I would not place my hope in a specific outcome, but I would put my hope in you. I pray that I would experience the fullness of joy that comes in your presence, the peace that surpasses understanding.

Continue praying in your own words …

Questions for Reflection:

1. What is your "Still Waiting" story?
2. In what ways did you think "if only" God showed up according to your timeline/plan that your story would be different?
3. How does it impact you to consider the nearness of Jesus amid your deferred hope?
4. How does honesty with God help us in our relationship with Him?

Chapter Two: Edges of Trust

I imagined our referral call a million times. I naively pictured goosebumps and butterflies. Over and over again, I heard the same story from adoptive parents: the first time they saw their child's photo, they just knew. *Well, that's something to look forward to!* I thought. I imagined feeling connected to the child's name or story and a feeling of capability with any special needs. Our new social worker, Amelia, called. My heart drops. Could this be *the* call?

Muffled sounds, lousy connection, I can barely hear Amelia on the other end. Something about a child, Amelia couldn't recall the name. It felt like a fuzzy fast-food drive-thru order. Amelia was driving and didn't have all the info yet. She tried twisting her phone in a different direction to read the details.

Is this our referral? Is this the call we've

been waiting for? Everything about the call felt wrong, and every fiber of me wanted it to feel right.

After Amelia pulled up to her destination, she read a few more details. She agreed to bring the file to our house the next day to discuss it. The more we prayed about it, the more uneasy we felt. We couldn't ignore the pit in our stomachs. It wasn't a good match for our family. I wondered if it was a mistake. *Was this referral meant for a different family? Did they look at our file at all?* (I wish I could share details, but due to child confidentiality, I can't.) Not only was this child the wrong fit for our family, but we also knew our family was not a good fit for the child's needs either. Confusion swirled around us. We waited years for this moment, but it wasn't at all what we expected.

Our former social worker moved on to a new career, so when Amelia came to our house the next day, it was our first time meeting her. The minute she sat down, she said to us enthusiastically, "So, are you guys excited?!"

I didn't know what to say. My husband and I both looked at each other, stone-faced. We knew this wasn't right. We knew we could not adopt this child; God had another family for them.

We shared our feelings with Amelia, and she understood. After spending time getting to know us, she agreed this referral was not a good fit. She made many notes in our file, determined to ensure a better fit for the next referral.

We wondered how it would feel to be in this position - saying no to a child. We assumed we'd never have to. But God gave us an indescribable peace about this decision. We were not saying no to this child; we were saying yes to God. We were saying yes to HIS plan, both for our family and for this child.

We didn't realize declining a referral was a *big* no-no. Even though our agency assured us it was not a problem, it left the entire adoption hanging by a thread. Like a protective birth mother, the country wasn't sure they wanted to work with us anymore. They would discuss further and let us know.

This whole situation required us to have a difficult conversation with our adoption agency. They didn't educate us on any special need's definitions. They told us we could request the gender (we found out after this attempted match, you cannot). They told us if we asked for a sibling set on our application, we'd be matched with one. Lastly, we had no idea it was frowned upon to decline a referral. *Why, after years into the process, were we just learning all this?*

We were well educated for post-placement

challenges but uninformed about the matching process. There were many things we wish we knew from the start. We considered changing paths. Maybe this wasn't the right avenue of adoption for us after all. But we were so far in, paid all the fees, waited this long. We couldn't help but wonder, *did we just mess up the whole thing?*

Laughing at the Impossible

After our failed referral, I felt so anxious I laughed. And I wondered if that's how Sarah from the Bible felt when she heard she would have a baby at ninety years old. The three prophetic visitors in Genesis said Abraham's wife would have a baby in a year. Sarah, listening from inside the tent, laughed to herself. "After I have become shriveled up and my lord is old, will I have delight?" (Gen. 18:12) In modern-day translation; *"Yeah right."*

I can relate. Our situation seemed impossible. If the country will still work with us, we either take whatever child(ren) they present to us (whenever that may be) or decline and risk losing all our money, time, and the chance of ever adopting in that country again. All that wait and work, potentially for nothing. But what if the match wasn't right for our family?

What if it seemed risky for our biological kids? I felt stuck in a corner. We'd come so far … waited so long.

I remember sitting on the back patio, head in hands, laughing to God. I wanted to cry, but instead, I laughed. I have a habit of laughing when I feel nervous, and I don't know what to do. My family teases me, but it's a curse. I've laughed at funerals, during arguments, during door-to-door sales pitches, and when people (including my children) fall. It sounds like I'm a terrible person, but I'm telling you it's uncontrollable. The only upside is that Brandon and I never can argue much because I start smiling and laughing, and it breaks all the tension. "This isn't a real smile right now. I don't think this is funny," I'll tell him, trying to get back to the issue at hand. But it's hard to stay angry when you're smiling and laughing, even if it came from some abnormal stress response. That silly nuance might be the secret to our happy marriage.

On the patio that day, I said out loud, "Lord, this feels like you're taking me to the very edges of my trust in you." I felt like Tom Cruise in one of the "Mission Impossible" movies, when he's hanging on to the edge of a cliff with only a finger or two.

"This is it, God. This is all I have to give. You have every ounce of my trust; there isn't a drop left."

I prayed. What else could I do? I kept praying and surrendering, day after day, asking God to expand the borders of my capacity to trust Him. Or maybe my last drop was enough. I wasn't sure what to make of it. I prayed a lot for God to guide the hands of the social workers. I prayed prayers to control the outcome, like piecing together the end of a novel, shuffling plotlines around to determine the best ending. Then I'd surrender it all and later start shuffling again. It was a bit of a mess, really. But something broke loose every time I talked to God this way - real, raw, vulnerable, full of the range of emotions I know Jesus experienced when He walked on the earth. I wasn't hiding anything, even my quirky need for control. I just laid it all at His feet ... and if I happen to pick it back up again, I'd bring it back, like a dog who thought we were playing a game of fetch.

Elisabeth Elliot writes, *"God is God. If He is God, He is worthy of my worship and my service. I will find rest nowhere but in His will, and that will is infinitely, immeasurably, unspeakably beyond my largest notions of what He is up to."* [ii]

Sarah laughed because she knew she couldn't make it happen herself. The promise from God was too big, too far-fetched. I mean, the lady is 90 years old and in menopause. (That's pretty close to impossible, from what I understand.) I think Sarah accepted her fate as a barren woman in a culture that shamed barrenness. I also wonder if Sarah laughs because she's too heartbroken to even think of intimacy with her husband. After all, twice Abraham lied, passing Sarah off as his sister, exposing her to possible sexual violation, while he stands by with nothing to say. Not to mention, Sarah watches Abraham finally have a son - but it's not with her, it's with her handmaiden, Hagar. The desire of her heart toddles before her day after day, but the child doesn't belong to her. The child belongs to Abraham and Hagar. It seemed like a good idea at the time, building a family through Hagar -- but now it only serves as a daily reminder of her barrenness.

And yet, despite all the obstacles ...
Despite the fact that Sarah was 90 years old,
Despite the raw spots in her marriage,
Despite all of her wounds and pain,
Despite her doubt and fear,
Despite her taking the plan into her own hands with Hagar,
Despite her harsh and jealous treatment toward Hagar,

Despite her hopelessness and lack of faith ...

God fulfilled His promise, and Sarah gave birth to Isaac.

It would be great if Sarah paved a road for us all to follow, a road of faith and optimism and kindness and trust. Wouldn't it be great if she gave us the formula to follow for our waiting season? I can see it in the headlines: "Faith-Filled Woman Gives Birth in Her Nineties." We'd all lean in for that kind of faith. Give us the formula. Only there isn't one.

The truth is, Sarah wasn't all that full of faith. She didn't play all her cards right. Sarah wasn't always pleasant or kind or an embodiment of the fruits of the Spirit. And it seems to me, the action she took only made things messier than they needed to be. Yet, God still fulfilled what He promised. We don't prefer this narrative because we seem to have a habit of looking for perfect people in the Bible to emulate. We build five-point sermons around these people, and there's nothing wrong with that as long as we remember; they are human, just like you and me. Jesus is the only perfect one.

I seldom shared adoption updates because a part of me felt embarrassed. I wondered if the long wait was somehow my fault. We picked the wrong agency, we chose the international route, we declined a referral. I stacked evidence against myself to prove that if I shared my "still waiting" updates, people must be eye-rolling on the inside, thinking the same thing I was thinking, *she must be doing something wrong.* What made me pause is that I would never want any of my friends to feel that way about their waiting season. And biblically, I didn't see a works-based formula for a short wait.

If everyone got exactly what they wanted through trust and surrender, we'd rejoice because we finally nailed the formula. Surrender isn't because God needs something from us but because He wants something for us -- the peace that comes through cutting off all that tethers our soul to anything but Him. Surrender and trust enable us to accept the outcome, even if it looks different than we thought it would.

We don't earn God's promises through patience. For those who insist on letting their ego lead, this isn't good news. They want to trust in their righteousness, their faithfulness, and their perfect performance. They see their spiritual 4.0 GPA as evidence of how much they deserve God's blessings and how the inferior does not. They are the mall cops of righteousness, pointing out all the specks in everyone else's eyes while ignoring the plank in their own.

For those of us honest enough to admit how often we mess things up, it makes us let out a sigh of relief. It's God's grace, not our effort. It's God's plan, not our perfection. We are not the hero of the story; God is the hero.

God cannot be shrink-wrapped to fit in our boxes. His thoughts are not our thoughts; His ways are not our ways. We cannot sift God's ways down to a one-size-fits-all formula for our desired outcomes. But we still try, don't we? God bursts the seams open every time, leaving us scratching our heads. Will we trust Him anyway, even if our little game of God-in-the-Box never works?

I don't want to put my trust in myself, in my plan, in my perfection. I don't want to put my trust in my desired outcome. I don't want to put my trust in my feelings. I don't want to put my trust in my perception of my righteousness. I want to put my trust in Christ alone. I might wage war with my pride by the hour. I might continue to be like the dog playing fetch, continually surrendering the same thing over and over. I might be like Sarah, missing the bullseye. But Sarah is living proof that our perceived mistakes and imperfections don't hold as much power as we think.

A Prayer for Those Who Need Trust:

Father, forgive me for lacking trust in you. Forgive me for trusting too much in myself, my capabilities, my circumstances, or others. Help my full trust to reside in you. I surrender my doubt, my fear, and my confusion. I don't know where this path leads, but I want to trust you every step of the way. When my heart wanders, pull me in. When my faith wavers, steady my soul. When my mind spins, bring me peace. Thank you for a new level of trust in you.

Continue praying in your own words …

Questions for Reflection:

1. Have you had your on-the-edges-of-trust moment yet?
2. What stands out to you about Sarah's story?
3. Have you ever wondered if you messed the whole plan up?
4. Do you struggle to try to control the outcome of your waiting season? What helps?

Chapter Three: Contentment

On May 31st, 2019, we loaded our belongings in a seventeen-foot trailer, Florida bound. Technically, the trailer was longer than seventeen feet, but we paid for precisely seventeen feet of use and used every square inch, all the way to the brim. We tetrised our bikes, our throw pillows, our kids' toys, our clothes hangers, tossing out anything that didn't fit.

We were moving. Across the Country. This was happening. What started as a playful *what if* conversation, ended up becoming a reality. We threw around the idea of lower taxes, living closer to Brandon's parent's retirement home, linking arms with our mentors in their marriage ministry, a slower pace of life, and switching Brandon to a remote position. After a while, it all started to make sense. (Tack on seven dreams about living in Florida, and this spark of an idea formed into a blazing fire.) We could not get Florida out of our heads. After taking a trip to Disneyworld and snorkeling in the warm Atlantic Ocean, our kids couldn't get Florida out of their heads either.

We hired a moving company to drive the truck for us, allowing us to use our car to road trip from San Diego, California (population 1.4 million) to Hobe Sound, Florida (population >14,000). We refer to this road trip as one of our favorite family memories that we never want to repeat.

Our first stop was Tucson, Arizona. I planned our lodging strategically but left room in the itinerary for spontaneous fun or rest. I wasn't sure how tired we'd be from all the driving. Up until this point, our furthest family road trip was only three hours. We were complete road trip rookies attempting to drive across the country.

Driving away from California felt surreal. We drove away from the dreamy California coast to a dry, rocky desert. Many areas felt like ghost towns, and, as usual, Brandon wanted to stop and explore every one of them. We listened to the Swiss Family Robinson audiobook, the narrator's voice lulling us all to sleep (except the driver, of course). The sun beat down on the rocky mounds, shadows casting across the road in stripes. The rock formations felt like driving through caves. The hues of brown land

and rocks rotated as the clouds shifted, a kaleidoscope in the desert.

The roads were barren and blank, some might see it as a bad thing, but I saw it differently. Bare and blank are full of possibility, the perfect foundation to build anything you want. I don't see dead and dry; I see a clean vastness of soil, ready to plant and water. But desert seasons, though full of promise, aren't easy.

Our youngest asked to go horseback riding, and Tucson seemed like the perfect place for it. After getting settled in our lodging, we drove forty-five minutes to the ranch. When our GPS indicated we were close, I remember thinking, *who could live in a place like this? It's so far outside of town! What is there to do? I could never be content living out in the middle of nowhere.*

We turned a corner and saw logs shaped into a fence. The sign at the entrance read, "Vaya Con Dios," with two iron horses on each side of the top of a curved arch. I took a picture of the sign, unaware of its meaning. Brandon, who speaks Spanish, said "Vaya Con Dios" with his best accent. "Go with God."

Go with God.

I inhaled those words along with the warm Tucson air. As hard as it was to walk away from our season in San Diego, God placed this reminder on the first leg of our journey that He was right there with us. *Vaya Con Dios. Go with God. I think I will go with God. Thank you very much.*

As we pulled into the horse area, my kids were in heaven. While waiting for our guide, the kids reached right through the fence, petting the horses' noses and brushing their sides. A couple of mangy dogs snarled at us. The tour guide told us only one of them is friendly, but he didn't tell us which one.

Our guide was tall and gruff. He wore a cowboy hat, Levi's, cowboy boots, and a flannel that seemed too warm for the heat. He introduced himself as "Red." We assumed it was a nickname, but we didn't ask. Red was gentle with my kids as he helped them mount their horses. My kids quickly memorized the horses' names, Roxy, Bonehead, Bear, Eagle, and Frank. I got Bonehead. I accidentally kept calling him Butthead, but Red didn't think it was funny.

Red took us through the Tuscan terrain; our horses kept a slow and steady pace, following behind one another. My son's horse fit his personality, refusing to follow the set path. PJ's horse insisted on stopping to graze every few minutes, and that seemed fitting too. PJ looked back at me and said, "Mom, I rate this experience a 10 out of 10." Our journey is starting to feel like an adventure.

We stopped to take pictures and drink water and chat with Red a little more. Red told us this is a seasonal job for him. He spends half the year giving horseback tours in Arizona and the other half in Montana. He told us about the cold winters in Montana and how he used to ride horses professionally. After spending ten years in California, I formed a prediction. I assumed Red was about to complain about why he didn't make it as a rider and how this job was just a stepping stone. He'd complain about the heat, where he lived, his career, and how the glory days existed somewhere else.

"I used to be a rider," Red explained, "I'd travel 'round, competing and such. After a while, I was ready to settle down a bit. I've been doing tours fer fourteen years; it's gotta be 'bout the perfect job. I do what I love, teach others 'bout horses, I get to be out here in nature, and meet people like y'all from all over the world." Red took a deep breath as if savoring the moment.

"And the nights here … you can't beat 'em. It's so nice being this far out of town, far away from the noise. It's so quiet, so peaceful. You should see the stars out here at night. There's nothin' like it. I could sit outside here fer hours. Between here and Montana, I get the best of both worlds. I'm a lucky guy; I'm living my dream."

Red's words jolted my soul. He was genuinely grateful for his life, and even after doing the same job in the same places for over a decade, he still held a sense of wonder. I'd never met anyone so ... content.

The warm air dried up my tears before they grace my cheeks. Red embodied traits I admire without fanfare. He lives a simple life, he remains humble, he feels immensely grateful for God's beauty around him, and he loves using his passion to serve others. What more could anyone want out of life? I felt guilty for my earlier comment; *who could live in a place like this?* Someone perfectly content, that's who.

Red was a breath of fresh air for my soul. It took me back to my childhood for a moment. Do you remember when you were a kid, and every job seemed like a dream job? Just the very idea of having a job was a big deal. We'd pretend to be a baker, a teacher, a window washer, or a mailman. Everything was fun and exciting because, in our imaginations, we were grownups with *real-life jobs*. What could be more exciting than delivering that letter into the mailbox slot? I see this play out in my kids' lives.

Yesterday my oldest two children were dreaming about working at a grocery store together. They had it all planned out; one of them would be the cashier and the other a bagger. My son, who happens to be obsessed with growing up, already calculated how many years it will take for him to buy his first home with his grocery store income. His face lights up at the possibility of owning his own place one day. Their childlike wonder reminds me not to take anything in life for granted. My kids are God's beautiful reminder that I'm already living in answered prayers and realized dreams.

Red led us back down to the horse stables. We all sipped water and shook his hand one last time. The kids said goodbye to Roxy, Bonehead, Bear, Eagle, and Frank, patting each of them as new friends.

"Vaya Con Dios." He said, tipping his hat.

"Thank you. We will." I said before getting back into our car.

Beware of Food Poisoning

In the book of Ecclesiastes, we see

Solomon's quest to find the meaning of life. He tries everything -- pleasure, wine, wisdom, projects, achievement, slaves, silver, gold - you name it. Solomon eventually discovers what nags at our hearts, too: everything changes. Earthly things unravel. Nothing remains. Generations pass. Nobody remembers anybody. Kinda depressing, huh? You can almost hear the exhaustion of Solomon's soul when we read his words (1:14) *"I have seen everything that is done under the sun; and behold, all is vanity and a striving after the wind."*

Solomon is right. It *is* exhausting striving to find our worth and fulfillment at the world's buffet table. It is so exhausting that we forget to stop and ask why we're eating this crap to begin with.

After Solomon surveys it all, he concludes it was all meaningless, and the best way to spend our days is to fear God and enjoy life.

"There is nothing better for a man than to be happy and do good while they live. That everyone may eat and drink, and find satisfaction in all his work -- this is a gift from God." (Ecc. 3:12-13)

"Enjoy life with your wife, whom you love, all the days of this meaningful life that God has given you under the sun--for this is your lot in life." (Ecc. 9:8)

Waiting for something in life doesn't mean we have to wait to enjoy life. Solomon's conclusions hold extra weight because he achieved it all. He spared no expense in the pursuit of his endeavors. We don't need to feast at the world's buffet table because King Solomon already warned us about the food poisoning.

Content while Contending

1 Timothy 6:6 tells us that *"Godliness with contentment is great gain."* The NLT translation says it a little differently. *"Yet true godliness with contentment is itself great wealth."*

The apostle Paul speaks of the contentment he found in Philippians 4:11-13 *"I am not saying this because I am in need, for I have learned to be content whatever the circumstances. I know what it is to be in need, and I know what it is to have plenty. I have learned the secret of being content in any and every situation, whether well fed or hungry, whether living in plenty or in want. I can do all this through him who gives me strength."*

It's tempting to imagine Paul penning these words from a mountaintop; we must remember he wrote this from prison. Paul writes this letter as he's locked away from the church he loves and from the work that he's most passionate about. He writes while he's under the daily threat of execution. Paul writes with the intent of encouraging others to be content in all circumstances. He found the one thing no one could ever take from him, execution or not.

Our waiting seasons may look different, but we are on the same journey in many ways, trying to find the balancing act between contentment while contending for more. Content while contending. Sometimes I walk the tightrope well, and other times I tip over the edge of contentment into the land of comfort. Comfort is alright for a while until complacency creeps in. Complacency rubs his beer belly and stretches his arm around my shoulders. He says, "scooch in, sweetie," while he spills pizza grease on his already dirty t-shirt. Complacency leaves a big dent in my sofa, and the door shuts tightly to the outside world because it's all about me and no one else. I forget to serve, to lift my eyes to the needs of others. I fail to dream beyond my own pleasures.

Then there's the other side of the balancing act, contending. If I contend without the balance of contentment, I meet striving. Striving slithers through my veins, finding the nerve endings in my shoulders and neck before striking. Striving crawls through my belly, tightening every muscle. Striving uses God only as a genie-in-a-bottle because it's all about the controllable outcome. Striving turns everything into a triathlon I haven't trained for. It leaves me breathless and exhausted and, like Solomon says, chasing after the wind.

We can be content while contending for more; they are not mutually exclusive. It doesn't have to be one extreme or the other. Contentment isn't complacency, and contending isn't striving. God invites us to both; He invites us to be content in all circumstances, and He also invites us to knock and keep on knocking.

We hold out our balancing stick, wondering if the crowd below will watch us fall off this tightrope on one end or another. We cling to our hopes, trying to push away the fear of coming up empty-handed. My mentor, Julie, serves as a safe landing pad for my fears in our adoption journey. As I express my worries to her, she said to me, "Melissa, if it doesn't work out, God will give you the grace for it."

Julie's simple statement stuck with me. I often imagine worst-case scenarios on this journey of trusting God. *What if I trust Him, and it all fails? What if I lose all of what we've worked toward? What if ... What if ... What if?* Julie's words gave me a powerful weapon of truth to fight with. "Then God will give me the grace for it." I speak those words out loud, declaring contentment over my present and my future.

I think this is what Paul refers to when he says, "I can do all things through Him who strengthens me." (Phil. 4:13.) It doesn't mean we can do anything we want, and it will work out because we slapped on a scripture verse. It means, whatever circumstances come our way, God's strength will carry us through. He will not leave us to handle it all alone. No matter if it's the highest mountain top or the deepest valley, God will be there, offering His sweet grace.

Contentment isn't where we live or how much money we have. It's not near the ocean or in the desert (although I have a preference). We can find contentment, like Paul said, in every circumstance. And if we have both godliness and contentment, we can go ahead and consider ourselves filthy rich.

Contentment is contagious. After my interaction with Red, my shoulders relaxed. A person who found the secret to contentment holds power to impact everyone they interact with. It's almost as if they hand out invisible permission slips. We think to ourselves; *if that guy is content with a simple life under the stars, I can be too.*

I've read a lot about Blue Zones lately. Blue Zones are areas worldwide where people live the longest, regions where people consistently live past 100 years old. Regions like Ikanaria, Greece, Okinawa, Japan, Ogliastra, Sardinia, and more. Dan Buettner, the author of *Blue Zones* and *The Blue Zones Solution*, studied these unique communities' habits. What do they eat? How do they spend their time? What is the secret to eating and living like the world's healthiest people? In a nutshell: eat well, stress less, move more, and love more.[iii] It sounds similar to Solomon's advice, doesn't it?

In *The Blue Zones Solution,* Dan shares various encounters with Blue Zone individuals. With each personal story, he shares their counter-culture way of life. Some of them stop to take a siesta. Some of them work in their garden daily. Some of them slowly walk up and down the mountain slopes, shepherding their sheep. None of them have a gym membership. They aren't CrossFit elites. They share tight-knit communities, some of them committing to a small group of friends for life. They aren't famous or super-successful by American standards. One thing the centennials seem to share is contentment.

Many people tell themselves when they reach a certain destination, they'll be content. Once they have a baby, they'll be content, once they get married, land their dream job, have a certain amount of money in the bank, or retire. But once they meet the benchmark, they immediately create another. They receive one answer to prayer and quickly move on to the next. In a frenzy, their minds search for what's missing. They resemble Adam and Eve in the garden of Eden, focused on the one thing they don't have rather than all the gifts they do have.

Charles Spurgeon once stated, *"You say 'If I had a little more, I shall be very well satisfied,' You make a mistake. If you are not content with what you have, you would not be satisfied if it were doubled."*[iv]

When I think about the adoption, I don't want it to become another benchmark to contentment. Do I want another child? Of course. Do I feel drawn to adoption? Yes. Will I feel disappointed if it doesn't work out? Absolutely. But I remind myself of Julie's words, "If that happens, God will give me grace."

I can be content while still contending for more. I can be content and still pray that God brings the right child into our lives at the right time. I don't have to wait until I reach a specific benchmark to choose contentment. I can choose it right now, at this very moment.

Via Con Dios, Go with God.

A Prayer for The Discontent:

Father, forgive me for any discontentment I have in my heart. Please help me not to focus so much on what I don't have that I miss out on all your blessings. Help me to stay grateful and remain in awe of you and your beauty. Let the contentment I choose daily become contagious to others. Help me be content in all circumstances, and always remember you will give me grace for even the most challenging season. In my waiting season, help me find the balance of remaining content while I contend for more.

Continue praying in your own words …

Questions for Reflection:

1. What beauty is around you that you've taken for granted?
2. What answers to prayer are you living in right now?
3. Have you started to hyper-focus on what you don't have?
4. When you imagine your wait not ending in your desired outcome, does that picture include God's grace or God's absence?

Chapter Four:
Wrestle Through the Wait

As we entered New Mexico, the landmark that most excited us was the White Sands National Monument. The only problem? It required a detour. You know how I feel about detours. I calculated the amount of "lost time" we'd have to make up for - two hours. That might not seem like a lot, but when you're driving for a week straight, every delay feels unnecessary. But the pictures on the internet sing to us; the monument looked like mountains of snow. Then we see photos of people sledding down the sandhills. *Sand-sledding? I've never heard of such a thing.* I bit my lip. Isn't this what the big move was all about, learning to slow down, embrace detours, and enjoy the journey? *Maybe it will be worth the delay,* I concede.

  Two hundred seventy-five square miles of Gypsum sand sprawls out in rolling hills. Usually, gypsum dissolves in water, but because this area is so dry, it remains preserved, tossed around very slowly by the wind, like waves in the ocean. As we pulled in, the woman at the visitor's center handed us a map. I wonder what we needed a map for, but when I looked at it, I understood. Townlike, the different driving paths loop between the sandhills. Instead of houses, this town holds mounds of snow-like gypsum. The gypsum piles up so high in certain parts that it partially covers the tall road signs. For a moment, it feels like we stepped onto another planet; everywhere we turn, there is a sea of white sand with a cobalt blue backdrop.

  I expected the sand to be scorching hot, but gypsum doesn't absorb heat from the sun, unlike regular sand. We took our dog, Henry, off the leash and let him run free. He raced up the hills and back down, tongue flapping out of the side of his mouth. I slipped my sandals off and dug my feet into the cool sand while the kids raced up the hill with their sleds. A couple of families picnic at the bottom while others take pictures of their kids sledding down the dunes. Brandon put on sunscreen while I followed the kids to the top of the hill. I knew I'd get sand in my shorts, but I couldn't miss the chance to go sand sledding with my kids. After all, when does anyone go *sand sledding?*

The sand wasn't so bad; it trickles right out of my shorts when I reached the bottom of the hill. My husband was reluctant to go down the hill; he has a bit of an aversion to excess sand in places it's not supposed to be. For our beach trips, Brandon is the one that makes sure every item goes in a specific pocket in our beach bag, so we don't drag any unnecessary sand back into the car or the house. He ensures we wash our feet or bodies off in the outdoor showers before we get in the car, and if we have any remaining sand on our feet, we have to "hose off" before we go in the house. He's quite obsessive about it, and it drives him nuts that I always seem to have extra sand in my swimsuit when I get back home. He finds the evidence on our bathroom floor and lovingly points it out.

I begged Brandon to come down the hill with us. "When else are we going to get to go sand sledding?" Despite his iffy feelings towards sand, he couldn't resist a call to carpe diem.

Brandon made the mistake of not letting his sunscreen dry before he sled down the hill. His sled doesn't hold him up the whole way down, and he rolled down the hill like a ball of cookie dough rolling in sugar. I called him my sugar cookie for the rest of the day. The kids don't understand why Mom can't stop laughing but watching Brandon wrestle trying to get the sand off his body made my stomach cramp up.

"It won't come off." He said as he tried scraping the sand off his arms using his hands and a towel. He flicked his arms and furrowed his brow. He wanted every grain of sand plucked from his skin as soon as possible.

"It's not coming off!" He shouted, flailing like he's getting attacked by a swarm of flies.

"Well ... you sparkle now, honey. It's a pretty look on you, really."

He gives me a side-eye with a cracked smile. This alone, I decided, was worth the two-hour detour.

Our car's glittery interior was evidence of our epic trip to the White Sands Monument, but most especially on the driver's side.

Walking With a Limp

Texas was the next stop on our endless road trip. We visited family in Fort Worth and Nanny (Jenna) in Houston. Life in Texas certainly felt different than San Diego; the large yards, the expanse of land, the space in between everything. Nanny's house was a great resting point where we had the margin in our trip to stay a few days. Curling up on her couch, drinking hot tea, watching the kids swim in her pool, it all felt therapeutic. Nanny always has this effect on me.

Nanny is one of those people you can be yourself around. There's no pressure to perform, no need to entertain. She's just as content out exploring as she is on the couch snuggled up watching Hallmark movies. We laugh together and cry together in the same half-hour. She whips up homemade sourdough bread or another delicious recipe from her Irish or English roots and makes it look easy. If I want to vent about something, there's room to vent. If I were to say something off-color (not that I ever do that), she wouldn't judge me for it. Our faith perspectives are different, but we focus on our similarities rather than our differences.

Even though Nanny is as holy as any Mormon I've ever met, she still takes me by surprise sometimes. She'll show up with a diamond on her tooth or a piercing in an unexpected place, or she'll tell us all a saucy little joke about saggy boobs or wankers. She keeps us all on our toes, and we love it.

I talk to Nanny a lot about the adoption; she's walked with us from the very beginning.

"I would have had another baby!" I told Nanny. "If I would have known it would take this long, I would have had another baby." I sighed deeply as Nanny provided a safe space for me to share freely.

Brandon got a vasectomy years ago because we were convinced the adoption was right around the corner. I'm not complaining. I realize some couples would love to be in our shoes with three biological children. But when I browse through old pictures of my kids on my phone, I meet the prick of disappointment once again. I'm not ready to close the chapter on little ones yet.

Nanny shared how excited she is to be a Nanny all over again. She talked about hanging a Christmas stocking up for my long-awaited adopted kids and I told her it will make me cry just like the first time I saw my name on her mantle.

Even though our conversation was going great, Nanny still seemed a little off. She typically hugs us a lot. She's squishy. She'd hate me for saying that because she'd assume I was talking about her thighs or something, but what I mean by squishy is that she's like a teddy bear. She's so lovely you can't stop hugging her. This time she seemed distant. There weren't many hugs or "I miss yous." But I wondered if it was all in my head since I'm not feeling well.

A couple of days passed, and I still couldn't shake the feeling that something was off. *Maybe I did something to offend her? Maybe I said something that hurt her feelings?* I needed to make it right, especially if I'd unintentionally caused pain.

We sat at the barstools one morning, drinking our coffee and nibbling on her homemade sourdough bread. Since it was just her and I, I decided it was the best time to bring it up.

"Hey Mom, can I ask you something?'

"Yes, of course, you can. What's up?" Nanny put her plate down.

"I just want to make sure I didn't say or do anything to offend you. Did I?"

"No, of course not. What would make you say or think that?"

"You just don't seem like yourself since we got here. You're usually more lovey, huggier. I don't know; maybe it's in my head."

"Wow, I guess you're right. I didn't think about how that would come across. Well, you know I had my hip surgery a few months ago. I have to wear this uncomfortable brace, and I can't cuddle with it. It also hurts if anyone bumps up against it, so I suppose I feel like I have this invisible shield around my body to protect myself. I'm also on these pain meds, and boy, they just make me feel so fuzzy in my brain. Have you ever felt like that? Like you just weren't yourself? But I guess you just have to keep going."

Nanny and I talked about how certain medications can suck the life out of you, make you not feel like yourself, and how people on the outside can't see that. Here I thought I did something wrong. Nanny was on her own journey of waiting, waiting for her body to heal. Waiting to feel like herself again, waiting to get back to loving and cuddling the way she used to.

Staying at Nanny's house made me want to light candles and tell everyone to book a flight. Let's all go to Nanny's for Christmas! Let's bake in the kitchen, let's go for a swim in the pool, let's go on walks around the pond, let's watch Hallmark Christmas movies, and watch the kids play with the dogs! But even though my family was at Nanny's, my whole family wasn't. It's a strange feeling to sit around a table knowing someone is missing.

There are moments when I think about my future adopted children, and I feel a sense of excitement and wonderment. Then there are moments when their absence feels heavy; they are too far away, and I feel helpless to change that. When you've done all the paperwork, you've signed every document, and you've prayed every prayer, what else can you do? Like David says in Psalm 39:7, *"And now, O Lord, for what do I wait? My hope is in you."*

Like Nanny, you keep going. You push through the painful moments, and you keep going. When you are waiting for something that can't be rushed, what other choice is there? You hope the people around you won't take it personally when they see you walking with a limp, when you're afraid to get too close, or you don't always have the right words.

Maybe there are moments in our waiting season that we can't give people what we gave them in the past. The margin isn't there like it used to be; maybe it's financial, emotional, spiritual, physical, or relational--we wish we had more to give, but we are still wrestling through our wait. It's not a permanent season, but we're still learning how to provide ourselves with what we need in this new season, let alone the people around us.

I burned my hand on a piece of pizza once. I know it doesn't sound like much, but my hand slipped straight into the scorching hot pizza sauce, fresh out of the oven. It was Superbowl Sunday and while everyone had fun, my throbbing fingers consumed my thoughts. I tried engaging fully in conversation. I tried paying attention to the game. I tried smiling and having fun, but my hand kept redirecting the attention straight back to the excruciating sting. I hoped I didn't come across distracted or cold to the people around me. I wanted to be fully present, but the pain limited my ability.

That little burn reminded me that everyone deals with unseen pain. Everyone wrestles with something. Our pain might vary from physical to emotional, but regardless, we could all use a little extra grace. The world would be a better place if we all believed the best about each other rather than jumping to conclusions.

I felt grateful for that conversation with Nanny. I could have bottled it up, assumed the worst, and left feeling jilted. Instead, our discussion opened the door for vulnerability and grace. I saw how much it hurt Nanny to be in the position she was in. Nanny's season of waiting is for physical healing; she can only do so much to speed up that process. She pushes through; she keeps making bread, serving her family, going to physical therapy. She's wrestling through her wait, wrestling with God, wrestling with her desire to move faster, wrestling through the fogginess of her medication. Have you ever had to wrestle through the wait?

Grappling with God

I once took my kids to try out a jiu-jitsu class.

I didn't know much about jiu-jitsu - I assumed we'd learn how to kick and punch like Charlie's Angels. *This will be fun.* We all dressed up in white kimonos and waited for our instructor on the dojo. The instructor assigned us partners and demonstrated the lesson. Before you know it, we are all on the ground with our partners twisted up like pretzels. Sweat on sweat, cheek to cheek (I won't tell you which cheeks). As I gasped for air, I locked eyes with my kids, their faces flush and speckled like watermelons, a combination of physical strain and embarrassment. They all got in the car, a little battle-worn and shell-shocked, and said, "Mom, can we please *never* go back?"

I learned a lot about wrestling that day. Wrestling is intimate. It's hard, strategic, tiring, and uncomfortable. It's not for the faint of heart or the easily embarrassed. But I also learned something I'll never forget. When the instructor walked around, examining our form, he said:

"95% of altercations end up on the ground. This is why we focus our efforts here. It's in these situations that you need to know what to do."

It makes a lot of sense. Hollywood kicks and punches might make me look cool, but if I want to know how to use this stuff in real life, the gritty groundwork is necessary.

If anyone from the Bible knows how to wrestle, it's Jacob. The scrappy fella came out of the womb grappling with his twin brother, Esau. Even though Jacob was described as a quiet man, let me tell you something I've learned about my quiet friends: don't assume they don't know how to fight.

Jacob, known for his striving and deceitful tendencies, also possesses a good trait: tenacity. Jacob fell in love, and he fell hard. Rachel, Laban's daughter, became the apple of Jacob's eye. Jacob loved Rachel so much he agreed to serve Laban for seven years in exchange for her hand in marriage. Genesis 30:20 tells us, *"So Jacob served seven years for Rachel, and they seemed to him but a few days because of the love he had for her."*

It seemed that Jacob's season of waiting went by in a flash; love made all those years of physical labor seem like a few days. But the night of the arrangement, Jacob wasn't presented with Rachel; Laban gives Jacob the oldest sister, Leah. Laban tricks Jacob and tells him that he'll have to serve him another seven years to receive Rachel. How would you feel if you got to the end of your season of waiting only to realize it doubled? Jacob spent fourteen years of his life toiling for the one he loved.

Jacob spends his life striving; it's what he knows how to do. He's gritty and resourceful, and he works situations to his advantage, even if it takes patience and perseverance. In Genesis 32:22-31, Jacob finds himself wrestling with God:

The same night he arose and took his two wives, his two female servants, and his eleven children, and crossed the ford of the Jabbok. He took them and sent them across the stream, and everything else that he had. And Jacob was left alone. And a man wrestled with him until the breaking of the day. When the man saw that he did not prevail against Jacob, he touched his hip socket, and Jacob's hip was put out of joint as he wrestled with him. Then he said, "Let me go, for the day has broken." But Jacob said, "I will not let you go unless you bless me." And he said to him, "What is your name?" And he said, "Jacob." Then he said, "Your name shall no longer be called Jacob, but Israel, for you have striven with God and with men, and have prevailed." Then Jacob asked him, "Please tell me your name." But he said, "Why is it that you ask my name?" And there he blessed him. So, Jacob called the name of the place Peniel, saying, "For I have seen God face to face, and yet my life has been delivered." The sun rose upon him as he passed Penuel, limping because of his hip."

Wrestling in our waiting season changes us

forever. For generations to come, the people of Israel don't eat the thigh's sinew on the hip socket because of Jacob's encounter. Jacob's wrestling not only changed his name and his identity, but it changed history.

Of course, by now, I hope you know I'm not talking about physically wrestling. I'm talking about the kind of wrestling that leaves your knees scraped and bruised because you've been on them so much. This kind of wrestling doesn't look like a rehearsed prayer or your Sunday best or the cross-stitch Bible verse hanging above your tulip arrangement. This kind of wrestling in prayer happens when we get gritty with God. When we finally ask Him the tough questions. It's intimate, it's face-to-face, real, raw, honest--and usually only happens when we are alone (unless you ugly-cry around other people, be my guest).

I'll never forget the first time I grappled with God. After my (birth) mom's funeral, I found myself back at my dad's place, sitting at his kitchen table wiping tears off my face.

Where is God in moments like this?
Does He care? Does He exist?
Does He see my pain?
Is there a plan in all this?

Many questions filled my mind while anguish filled my heart.

Suddenly, I felt the urge to pray. I never prayed before. Of course, I said 'Amen' at the end of someone's Thanksgiving prayer, but I hadn't ever prayed a sincere, on-my-own prayer.

I didn't know how to pray or if there was an appropriate way to approach God. *Do I start my prayer with Thee, Thou, or Dear Heavenly Father? Do I need to introduce myself? If so, did God need to know my first and last name? He already knew that, didn't He?*

I figured if God existed, He surely knew my name and my rookie status at prayer.

"God," I said as a salty tear hit my lips, "I am hurting right now. Please, if you are real, show me a sign. Show me everything is going to be okay."

I knew the "show me a sign" prayer probably wasn't the best approach, but in this instance, I hoped God cared more about the brokenness of my heart than the brokenness of my prayer. I felt anxious for a glimpse of hope on the other side of pain. But nothing happened. I remained in the same room with the same pain. I took a deep breath and wondered if it was all pointless. *Perhaps prayer is a waste of breath.*

After finishing my first rocky prayer, my dad's Yukon growled as it pulled into the garage, then grew quiet. I heard the door creak behind him as he walked in. I wiped the tears on my sleeves and straightened up to greet him. He said hello and dropped the stack of mail on the kitchen counter. On top laid a bright pink square envelope; he picked it up and tossed it onto the table right in front of me.

"Sorry, I kept forgetting to bring this home to you. Someone sent it to my office a while ago." He said before walking out of the room.

My name adorned the pink envelope, along with my dad's work address. The sender didn't write a return address in the corner; I had no clue who it was from. I tore open the envelope to reveal a swirly heart pattern on the front of a card. It was a Valentine's card. Six weeks passed since Valentine's Day; the holiday felt lost in a sea of painful memories. A lot happened since then; my mom died, they arrested the man responsible for her death, he committed suicide in prison, I attended her funeral, and I finally dragged myself back to school. An old Valentine's Day card seemed irrelevant to my new reality, but I opened it anyway.

The card read:

*I know we don't always see things eye to eye,
but we always see them heart to heart.
I will always love you,
and I am so proud of you, my little lamb.
Love,
Mom*

Tears spilled over the card and onto the table while my mind spun. Six weeks. 42 days.

For 42 days, that pink card from an unknown source sat somewhere in my dad's office. But on this day and this hour, he remembered to bring it home to me; the moment after I offered up my first broken prayer. My mom was dead, and I thought I'd never get the chance to hear "I love you" or "I'm proud of you" from her again. God orchestrated the perfect delay so I could live my life with written proof that my mom loved me and was proud of me. Everything else was water under the bridge.

Rising from the table that day, I knew three things for certain:

I knew despite the whirlwind of tragedy; I was going to be okay.

I knew, with every fiber of my being, God answered my first raw prayer.

And I knew I now lived in a new reality: *God was real.*

Grappling with God is unforgettable. It changes us in ways our rainbow days don't. This isn't choreographed kickboxing at the local gym. This is the real-life, gritty altercation that ends up on the ground. Most often, we wrestle with God because His presence and His promises feel far away. But what if it's the opposite? There is no such thing as long-distance wrestling.

There are times, like Jacob, when we can spin situations to our advantage. We can toil and labor, twist and take things into our own hands. Then there are times that what we seek cannot be satisfied by earthly means. We feel cornered, and our only choice is contending with God. Like Nanny, we find ourselves stuck. There's nothing we can do to speed up our healing or our waiting process. We need to be patient, keep wrestling with God, and keep walking with a limp.

In my experience, wrestling with God isn't only about a raw relentlessness in prayer but also a raw relentlessness with truth. When the truth of God's goodness doesn't feel true, are we willing to wrestle with it until it does? When our waiting season begins to define us, are we willing to grapple for a firm identity in Christ?

I once took sticky notes with verses about my identity and posted them all around my bedroom. None of them felt true, not a single one. I walked around my room, looking at the verses like a gallery in a museum. These verses seemed far off, someone else's artwork that I could only admire at a distance. But, like Jacob, I found some tenacity. I prayed each verse over myself before moving on to the next. And I did it again and again. Verses such as:

John 1:12 ~" *Yet to all who did receive him, to those who believed in his name, he gave the right to become children of God."*

John 15:16 ~ *"You did not choose me, but I chose you and appointed you so that you might go and bear fruit—fruit that will last—and so that whatever you ask in my name the Father will give you."*

Jeremiah 1:5 ~ *"Before I formed you in the womb I knew you ..."*

1 Peter 2:9 ~ *"But you are a chosen people, a royal priesthood, a holy nation, God's special possession, that you may declare the praises of him who called you out of darkness into his wonderful light."*

John 15:15~ *"I no longer call you servants, because a servant does not know his master's business. Instead, I have called you friends, for everything that I learned from my Father I have made known to you."*

Ephesians 2:10~ *"For we are God's masterpiece, created in Christ Jesus to do good works, which God prepared in advance for us to do."*

Psalm 139:14 ~ *"I praise you because I am fearfully and wonderfully made; your works are wonderful, I know that full well"*

    At first, the verses stayed surface deep as I wrestled with my identity. But I kept wrestling. I wasn't going to stop grappling with the truth until it moved from my head to my heart. If this is true -- all that I profess to believe -- then it isn't enough for me to know it academically; I want to know it personally.

    The process didn't happen overnight, but it

did happen, and it taught me how to wrestle relentlessly in prayer. It taught me never to settle for a comfortable lie when I have the power to replace it with a hard-won truth. And in our adoption journey, I gained a lot more practice. I discovered there are times when prayer feels like a gentle breeze, and there are times when prayer feels like a ruddy grappling match as relentless as my sugar-cookie husband scuffing sand off his body.

A Prayer for Those Wrestling

Father, thank you that I can come to you at my very worst. Thank you for accepting all of me. Father, thank you that you make yourself known deeply through these seasons of wrestling and waiting. Thank you that we don't stay the same because of these times; you make us more like you. Please help me to press into you during this time. Change me, Lord. Let my hope reside in you. I give you my heart's desire; there is nothing man can do. Help the truths I know move from my head to my heart as I wrestle with you in prayer.

Continue praying in your own words …

Questions for Reflection:

1. Have you ever felt like you were waiting to feel like yourself again?
2. What stands out to you about Jacob wrestling with God?
3. What does it mean to you to grapple with God in prayer?
4. What grace do you need to extend to yourself in this season?

Chapter Five: Weary in the Wait

After our restful stop in Texas, we toured a swamp in Louisiana, stopped for lunch in New Orleans, and stayed at a sketchy Airbnb in Tallahassee. It is the last leg of our trip, and our kids finally start to ask the infamous road-trip question, "Are we there yet?" I'm surprised it didn't happen sooner.

Every state we passed through held its own beauty, but once we crossed into Florida, there was a different air about it (and it's not just the humidity). Maybe it was my internal navigation system knowing we were closer to the ocean, but I felt like I could breathe deeply and settle in. I wouldn't say Florida felt like home immediately, but it felt like where we were supposed to be. We drove through draping trees that kissed at the tips and gazed at the farms framed by marsh. We stopped at a gas station with a bathroom nicer than The Hilton. To add to the confusion, a wild chicken roamed around the parking lot, and four shirtless dudes sat in the bed of a pickup truck. *We are not in California anymore.*

The exit for Hobe Sound caught our eyes, and our hearts leapt. Our new little town was around the bend; our anticipation was sky-high. We bought our house site-unseen (if you needed further proof of how crazy we are), so we held our breath a little. We rounded the corner with our stomachs in knots. Even though it was raining, the rain let up just for this moment.

"Welcome Home," our navigation said to us, and we all squealed at the irony. There have never been more exciting words spoken from Google Maps.

The kids raced to pick out their rooms, and we chose the room we wanted our future adopted children to share. For traumatized kids, nights can be the worst, so we decide that having them sleep close to our room made the most sense. We are ready for our babies … as soon as we complete another home study. I feel exhausted at the very thought of it.

The Gentleman

A couple of months after we moved to Hobe

Sound, I had a dream. Only my closest friends know how much I dream. I joke that my mind is too cluttered during the day, so God waits until I'm knocked out to speak to me.

In the dream, a tall gentleman stands before me. He feels familiar, safe, and trustworthy, like a friend I'd known my whole life. The tall gentleman reaches out and offers a hand to me. I know the man loves me; I feel it. He wants me to take his hand and be his forever. But he is just too familiar, and I reject him.

The dream flashes to me sitting at a table with friends. A short, stocky man approaches the table. This man makes it clear he's interested in me. He is aggressive, a fast talker with swagger. I am intrigued by this man; I get sucked in like a used car salesman telling me the offer is about to expire. I follow him -- in a flash, we are an item. He comes on strong; he doesn't take no for an answer. I push him off of me. He keeps trying to make me compromise, but I tell him no. His anger escalates, and he eventually storms out.

I feel manipulated and violated and deserted. I sit in a room alone, crying, craving the affection of someone who truly loves me.

At the end of the dream, I walk back up to the gentleman with tears in my eyes. I reached out my hand to him, and I say,

"I'm ready now… if you'll still have me."

The gentleman says, "of course," and he holds my hand. I feel safe again. I feel his deep love. It feels like safety and sunshine and protection and friendship. His hand is gentle and light; he leads me with grace, not force. We walk together, hand in hand, and I proudly introduce the love of my life to all the people who are most important to me.

I woke up and told my husband about my vivid dream. With tears in our eyes, we discussed the details, overwhelmed by God's love.

Jesus extends His love to me, and like a fool, I reject it for what appears more enticing. I choose the fast, the commanding, the striving, a spirit that won't take no for an answer. Only when I come to terms with the fact that the brute will never be pleased, do I realize where true love was all along, with the unforceful gentlemen, who never asked for anything but to love me.

When I return to the gentleman, I see him with new eyes. He's what I've looked for all along. He's not wrapped in swagger or pomp; He's humble and meek and full of love. Only when I accept His love can I introduce Him to others. All this time, it was that simple. No striving for a great ministry, no burning myself out to "do more for God." Only resting in His love am I able to proudly show Him off to others. He waited for me; He waited for this moment. He's never stopped loving me. I'm ready now.

I'm Ready Now

I can't get the dream out of my head. I'm ready now. I'm ready to stop the striving and the hustling. I'm ready to stop rushing through life. I'm ready to slow down, to rest, to let Jesus love me. I'm ready to savor life. I'm ready to learn how to wait well. Now is the perfect time to start, in a new sleepy little beach town where no one knows me.

When a woman accepts a proposal, she shows off her engagement ring proudly. After my dream, I feel like I accepted a proposal. I want to show off my commitment proudly.

"I want to change what I'm proud of," I told my husband one morning.

"What do you mean?" He asks

"I mean, I want to become proud of slowing down. Instead of priding myself in how productive and efficient I am, I want to take a season to become proud of myself for resting."

My husband seems skeptical; he knows me too well. But he likes the idea and tells me he's supportive. I get out a journal and record my progress.

I purchase blackout curtains, and I sleep in.
I'm proud of myself for sleeping an extra hour.
I block off time for a walk on the beach.
I'm proud of myself for going on a beach walk today.
I get a massage even though I feel guilty.
I'm proud of myself for getting a massage.
I prioritize and protect our weekends off.
I'm proud of resting this weekend.
I sit with Jesus by the pool and stare at the flowers.
I'm proud of myself for savoring today.

A few months go by, and we drive to South Carolina to stay at Brandon's parents' house. I rest in the rolling hills' beauty; I take walks daily; I stare at the red cardinals and their mates' building nests outside the window. I reflect on my tendency towards striving, my need to jump higher in order to work for God and His approval. It wasn't God's approval I was after; I already had that. I was coming to realize I have this desire to add something flashier to the finished work of Jesus much like a Pharisee. I read the gospels with fresh eyes, and I see many characters like me, spinning and toiling, trying hard to prove their worth. In Matthew 22, a sharpshooting Pharisee lawyer asks Jesus a question to try to test him.

"Teacher, which is the greatest commandment in the Law?"

And he said to him, "You shall love the Lord your God with all your heart and with all your soul and with all your mind. This is the greatest and first commandment. And a second is like it: You shall love your neighbor as yourself. On these two commandments depend all the Law and the Prophets."

I've spent most of my Christian journey with the mentality of this lawyer, *"What's next? What's the catch? Let's get down to business. What mountain shall I take? What's the greatest thing I can do for you? What can I do to speed this whole thing up?"*

Jesus doesn't shun me for my zeal, but He waits for me patiently. For those stubborn like me, we learn the hard way. His character and His pace are different from the world. He's a gentleman, and He won't force His agenda on us, but it's a simple one: love and be loved.

I keep wanting to pick up the heavy weight again out of habit, but He reminds me that He already fulfilled the Law; He already did the heavy lifting. It seems too extravagant, this free gift of grace and rest. It's a different way of living, ministry happening organically, God's love becoming the driving force and center of my life.

Rest, Wait, Listen, Renew

We made a friends with a man named Scott and his wife, Katharine. It felt like a big deal to have four friends in Florida. We met Scott at a John Maxwell Team event. Scott runs a successful landscaping business in South Florida. Despite his success, he's humble, never seems hurried, and always has a story to tell about how his pants fell down at the airport or the time he accidentally pinched the wrong person's butt. But the story that stands out the most is one Scott shares about learning to rest.

On September 19, 2016, Scott went to the doctor for a headache. Scott's doctor took his blood pressure and immediately sent him over to the medical center across the street. The medical team wasted no time. They performed a full craniotomy, scooping a massive amount of fluid from Scott's brain. After Scott came to consciousness, Scott's surgeon gave him the worst news he'd ever received.

The surgeon said, "Scott, you've come through the surgery amazingly. There's a chance you'll be okay, but here's what it's going to require. For the next eight weeks, you need to do everything in your power to let your brain settle down. You had a concussion when you had this brain bleed. The second concussion happened when we essentially took jackhammers and saws and cut your skull cap off. And then we went in and scraped your brain. So, you have to understand that it makes three major traumatic events for your brain. You will not read, write, communicate, or use your phone for the next eight weeks. You will not talk or have a conversation. You cannot watch T.V. or listen to music with lyrics. Your brain has to go flat ... and if you don't, you will have permanent brain damage."

When the surgeon walked out, Scott thought to himself, *I'm not afraid to die ... but I'm terrified of living like a vegetable my whole life. Given a choice, I would rather die.*

Scott went on, sobbing himself to sleep,

scared that crying might be too much for his brain.

How do I stare at the air for eight weeks? Lord, help me. Please give me a plan. Please, Lord, Give me a plan. Give me your plan. Scott prayed.

As Scott lay there, feeling helpless, God spoke to him. God answered his prayer and gave him a plan for the eight weeks. That plan involved resting, waiting, listening, and renewal. On the outside looking in, those eight weeks must have looked unproductive. Scott couldn't speak, couldn't write, couldn't read ... no television, no conversations, no browsing on the phone or computer. Absolute stillness for eight weeks.

Scott carried out God's plan each day, over and over again.

Rest. Wait. Listen. Renew.
Rest. Wait. Listen. Renew.

Day after day, Scott filled his mind only with God's plan to get him through the eight weeks. Rest. Wait. Listen. Renew. A deeper meaning formed around each word, a real understanding of what it meant to rest in God, to wait for Him, to listen to Him, and to be renewed by Him. Scott's body grew stronger and stronger each day. His brain slowly healed. He's a walking miracle.

To this day, Scott starts his morning the same way he filled his time during those eight weeks in the hospital. Rest. Wait. Listen. Renew. Every morning. Scott says, "I didn't know at the time that what God was teaching me would change me for the rest of my life. To this day, those four-morning practices are the key to any effective day running my business."

If anyone had an excuse to feel weary, question God, or flat out go crazy during a season of waiting, it's our friend, Scott. But he leaned into God's direction to rest, and it changed his life forever.

Weary in the Wait

Weariness in the wait brings out the worst in us. We have every excuse to be tired; we've waited a long time. The idea of throwing in the towel crosses our minds when we're weary. But the weariness wasn't meant to be worn. We don't want to drape weariness over our shoulders like a cloak of victimhood.

At dinner one night, I tell my family, "You know, I'm coming to believe that everything is fun when you aren't in a hurry."

We all have a good laugh around the table and agree with this statement. Cooking dinner is a drag when I'm trying to rush through it, but it's a different story when I turn on some music, take my time, and use the whisk as a microphone. The bottom line is, I like who I am more when I'm not rushed. I like who I am more when I'm taking the time to enjoy the process. I like who I am more when I'm not wearing weariness around like a badge of honor.

John Ortberg says, *"Biblically, waiting is not just something we have to do until we get what we want. Waiting is part of the process of becoming what God wants us to be."*[v]

I take a second look at the home study requirements. Instead of perceiving it as something I have to rush through, I decide to enjoy it as much as possible. If we need to get fingerprints again, let's make a date out of it and try out a new restaurant while we're out. If we have to fill out more paperwork, let's turn on music while filling it out. I've always thought the adoption timing was about external things; waiting for adoptions specialists, waiting to hear back from our agency, waiting for a referral, waiting until we finish our courses. But maybe the wait isn't about the logistics at all. Maybe

God's waiting on me, preparing and growing me from the inside out.

Perhaps there's still more detoxing to do from my fast-paced tendencies. My kids need a mom patient enough to see the pain behind the tantrums. They need a mom who gives them permission to express their hurt and be in process. I'm grateful for the people patient enough to stick with me while I sorted through my pain and trauma; people like Nanny never made me feel like I should be further along in my healing or my character. Nanny's steady and patient presence in my life cracked the door open for me to believe I was worthy of love, even if it took years to get there. I want to be that kind of person for others, especially for my kids. I want to take the garment of weariness and striving off and choose a better way, even if it is the slower way. I'm running a different race, one that relies on God's grace.

I feel ready every day. Ready to kiss my kids' little toes and stroke their hair. Ready to hear their laugh and toss them in the pool. I feel ready to kiss their cheeks and tickle their tummies. I feel ready to tuck them in at night and share our favorite board games and books. But God has a different definition of "ready" than I do. Maybe He was waiting for me to rest in His love, to accept His gentle hand. Walking hand-in-hand with God, and his slow pace, makes me wonder if my growth is just beginning. Strangely, that feels encouraging because at least it's somewhat within my control. It's not waiting on an agency or waiting on paperwork clearance or waiting for some social worker on the other side of the planet. Right here, at this very moment, I am not just waiting; I'm being transformed. It is not about the destination but about who I am becoming in the journey.

Pierre Teilhard de Chardin's poem from *"Hearts on Fire"* becomes a prayer:

Above all, trust in the slow work of God.
We are quite naturally impatient in everything to reach the end without delay.
We should like to skip the intermediate stages.
We are impatient of being on the way to something unknown, something new.
And yet it is the law of all progress
that it is made by passing through some stages of instability—
and that it may take a very long time.
And so I think it is with you;
your ideas mature gradually—let them grow,
let them shape themselves, without undue haste.
Don't try to force them on,

*as though you could be today what time
(that is to say, grace and circumstances acting on
your own good will)
will make of you tomorrow.
Only God could say what this new spirit
gradually forming within you will be.
Give Our Lord the benefit of believing
that his hand is leading you,
and accept the anxiety of feeling yourself
in suspense and incomplete.[vi]*

These are prayers I can pray because my children deserve a mom who isn't just ready for the lovely stuff, but one who's ready for the hard stuff too. I want to learn to trust in the slow work of God, both within myself and in others. My kids deserve a mom who knows how to rest, who can lead them to that person of rest, to Jesus, the gentleman, the one who gives us this amazing invitation in Matthew 11.

"Come to me, all you who are weary and burdened, and I will give you rest. Take my yoke upon you and learn from me, for I am gentle and humble in heart, and you will find rest for your souls. For my yoke is easy and my burden is light." Matthew 11: 28-30

Are you ready now?

A Prayer for The Weary

Father, thank you for being a gentleman. You are gentle and humble in heart, and you invite me to come to you when I'm weary and burdened. You lead me to a better way. You wait patiently for me. You don't manipulate or coerce. Help me to rest in you. Help me to become the kind of person who savors life with you. Make me more like you. Open up my eyes to the beauty in this journey of waiting, help me to draw closer to you, and to become more patient. Lord, help me to lay aside all striving and anxiousness. Your way is better. I'm ready now.

Continue praying in your own words …

Questions for Reflection:

1. In what ways do you feel weary in your wait?
2. What ways do you think God wants you to grow during this waiting season?
3. What stands out to you about Scott's story and his Rest, Wait, Listen, and Renew strategy?
4. What can you do this week to slow down and savor God's gifts?

Chapter Six: Staying Power

In case you didn't know, Florida summers are hot. I used to joke that I don't sweat much, but that was before I spent a full summer in South Florida. Back in San Diego, my husband and I went on morning prayer walks with our coffee in hand around the neighborhood. Shortly after moving to Florida, we grabbed our warm coffee and stepped outside.

How exciting, we get to go on morning prayer walks with our coffee in our new neighborhood!

Wow, it's hot.

Look at those pretty birds. Thank you, God, for the birds.

Why am I sweating so much?

The sun is so bright it hurts. Is there something wrong with my sunglasses?

I should ask Brandon if he wants to pray.

Dang, it's hot.

I'll grab his hand, then ask if he wants to pray.

Nope. Too sweaty.

Look at those pretty flowers. Thank you, God, for the beautiful foliage here.

Why don't I want this coffee? I love coffee.

It needs ice; that's what it needs.

This is okay. It's like a sauna. A free sauna.

I can't handle this.

You've only walked two blocks; suck it up.

Brandon just wiped his forehead with his t-shirt; I bet he's hot too.

"Hey, babe. Want to turn around?"

"Yep."

I can tell this story with a smile on my face because I love summers in Florida now. The best snorkeling is in the summer, and I love jumping in our pool after our beach days. But when we first moved here, we hadn't found our summertime stride yet. We tried imposing our year-round San Diego routine and failed miserably. That first summer, we drove up to Grammy's house in South Carolina for a week and almost gave up on Florida. South Carolina still has hot summers, but at least the mornings were cool enough to accommodate our coffee prayer walks. Walking around, enjoying a slight breeze again, we noticed ourselves looking around the neighborhood for homes for sale. The biggest thing that held us back from moving was not wanting to do a home study all over again. We told ourselves that the adoption was right around the corner; we couldn't move yet. But a big part of us wanted to run away and give up on all of it.

Around the same time, a friend of mine named Beth had also moved for a season. After giving birth to her second baby as well as being away from community, she feared another visit from postpartum depression. To stay vigilant, she asked for a couple of us to check in. At the time we would keep in touch through an app that enables us to leave each other video messages with another friend as well. A few weeks into the move, Beth's messages became increasingly emotional as she started working through some painful parts of her past. We welcomed her vulnerability, but we were concerned for her. We'd never seen this side of her, not even when she battled postpartum depression the first time. Through a cracked voice and tears, our friend's pain left us unsure about how best to support her. We offered up our hearts and homes, welcoming our friend to run away from her process. A couple of days went by, and we didn't hear from our friend. In the next video message from her, she bravely said,

"Guys, I know you love me. And the idea of running away right now sounds so tempting. But I know what God is doing in my life right now is for a reason. What I need right now is staying power."

Beth knew, despite the difficulty, that her season was healing deep wounds and wrong beliefs about herself. In her most challenging season of waiting to date, my friend found herself waiting for her hormones to regulate, waiting for God to renew her mind from wrong beliefs, waiting for life to return to normal and for healing to come in her heart.

Beth's words aided us in best supporting her, not by rescuing her out of her pain but by giving her a safe place to find strength within it. We encouraged her to keep going and told her how proud we were for her commitment to her health and well-being. As the months went by, the tearful messages from my friend became less and less. She continued to fill us in on her progress, and over those months, we watched a glimmer of hope shine through Beth again. Her cheeks glowed as she shared with us, "I feel joy for the first time in a long time. Simple, pure joy." When she eventually returned to San Diego, my friend's once tired eyes radiated with liberty and gratitude.

I wanted to rescue Beth from her painful process, but now I see she was right. Staying power was what she needed to step into freedom. She didn't need us to pluck her from her pain; she needed to keep putting one foot in front of the other and find strength within it.

Beth didn't know at the time how much I needed to hear her words—"staying power." I opened up to a different friend about my waiting season and the crazy Florida weather. The next day, my friend bombarded me with home listings back in San Diego and all the reasons why we should move back, including that it was most likely God's plan. It was tempting. I wanted to run back to the familiar, the comfortable--or at least somewhere I could drink my coffee outside in the mornings, dang it. I wanted someone to rescue me from all the unknowns of our new season. But what I needed was staying power.

Many times, in our season of waiting, well-intended people want to rescue us out of it. They feel confident in an alternative solution. They have it all mapped out in their minds. It may come at a time when you're already experiencing a pang of regret or doubt or discomfort. What the well-meaning people in our life need to know is that we are committed to God's path even when it's uncomfortable.

Staying power means we fully believe God

planted a seed in our heart, and we aren't going to give up until we see what it grows into. In his book *Draw the Circle*, Mark Batterson says, "Too often we pray ASAP prayers — as soon as possible. We need to start praying ALAT prayers — as long as it takes."[vii]

I appreciate Mark's perspective because stories about instantly answered prayer can discourage those who unceasingly pray for years and still come up empty-handed. You can preach to them all day long about persistence and the power of prayer, and they'll probably be nodding, smiling, and thinking *if you only knew*. Prayer is undoubtedly powerful, but this book isn't about God's *yes*, it's about God's *not yet*. It's about finding peace when *not yet* seems like it's the only answer you're ever going to hear. Mark's encouragement to pray ALAT prayers flips the script in our culture obsessed with instant gratification. It provides an empowering stance as if we take our corner in the ring of life and declare:

> *I'm not going anywhere.*
> *I'm going to keep hoping.*
> *I'm going to keep believing*
> *I'm going to keep praying.*

I'm going to stand firm in what I believe God spoke to my heart.

I'm going to let God continue to keep preparing me.

I'm going to trust in God's timing and not my own.

I'm here to stay.
I'm anchored in Him.
I'm not going anywhere.
I'm going to keep praying, As Long As it Takes.

The devil better watch out when a woman finds her staying power. She's not messing around anymore with temptations toward a more leisurely path; she's in it with God for the long haul. She's not letting anything or anyone sidetrack her from the vision in her heart. And even if the vision's timing is uncertain, you can count on her becoming her best while she's waiting for it.

Staying power is the heel-digging determination to let God finish the good work He started in us. Philippians 1:6 speaks of God finishing the work He started *in* us, but it also goes on to say that He will carry it on to completion until the day of Christ Jesus. So, basically, God is going to keep working on our character until Jesus comes back.

That's hardly a recipe for a speedy arrival point, but it is an invitation to continue to let Jesus make us more like Him.

Do good things come to those who wait? That might be true, but bare minimum, I believe that good things *are formed* in those who wait. Ecclesiastes 7:8 says, "The patient in spirit is better than the proud in spirit." Patience is the companion of humility and the antithesis of pride. When we chose patience, we choose Christ-likeness.

Maybe you thought a journey in patience would look like *The Sound of Music*, where we all sit around and sing songs about how content we are on the slow path. I'm here to tell you, at times, the waiting journey looks more like *Rocky Balboa*. There are moments when we've got to muster up a little Sylvester Stallone, put on our boxing gloves, and take his advice: "Life's not about how hard of a hit you can give... it's about how many you can take, and still keep moving forward."[viii]

Acceptance & Enjoyment

Staying power is the part of us that decides we aren't quitting or giving up hope, no matter how painful our process may be. But I think, after the zeal of staying power wears off, acceptance takes its place. Acceptance isn't any less resolved, but it is more settled. If staying power is Captain America, acceptance is Yoda. At first, acceptance feels like cough medicine; it's bitter sting slides down our throat as we try to embrace things as they are. But we're left with the sour aftertaste; through gritted teeth, we say, *"I accept this situation."*

I'm still waiting.

This is not where I thought I'd be.

If we refuse to live with resentment, we sit with God and acceptance long enough for the aftertaste to subside. Acceptance isn't settling into hopelessness; it's recognizing that God is God and I am not. It's embracing the simple truth that there is only so much within my control. It's unclenching my fists and using Psalm 46:10 as a pillow, *"Be still, and know that I am God."*

Acceptance surprised me by opening another

door, enjoyment. When I accept my reality and the things outside of my control, I am no longer defined by them. I've heard many stories about women who stopped looking for a spouse then found one. Or women who stopped trying for a baby then got pregnant. People throw around these stories like formulas. Somewhere along the way, I became less interested in formulaic tales and more interested in those who found peace and acceptance regardless of the outcome. The gifts of acceptance and enjoyment change my periods into commas.

I'm still waiting, but I'm enjoying the journey.

This is not where I thought I'd be, but life is still good.

I've heard that time flies when you're having fun. The problem is, I don't want time to fly. I don't want to push fast-forward in life to reach my end goal. But I don't want life to feel like waiting for a pot to boil either. Can we still have fun and not rush through life? Does it have to be one or the other, slow but tedious or fast but fun? When acceptance walked into the room and handed me enjoyment, it was a gift I wasn't expecting. It was a permission slip to savor life, enjoy the journey, and find meaning and purpose outside of completing my family. I watched Beth move through these phases, from staying power to acceptance to simple joy. She still waits for full inner healing, but she is no longer in a hurry. Her process is a part of her story, but it doesn't define her. She takes her kids on walks to the park, hosts dinner parties for her neighbors, and joined a new women's small group. She decided to still be in process while enjoying the process.

Isaiah 40:31 describes it like this:

"Those who wait on the Lord
Shall renew their strength.
They shall mount up with wings like eagles,
They shall run and not be weary,
They shall walk and not faint."

The Hebrew word that Isaiah uses for "wait" is Qavah. It means "to wait, look for, hope, or expect." This doesn't sound like an idle position. It sounds like the shift Beth made, where she stopped trying to resist the process and decided to grab hold of an expectant and determined staying power. It is waiting on the Lord that brings renewed strength. This Qavah means we wait for Him, look for Him, hope in Him, and expect His goodness.

Establishing our focus and fulfillment in

Him, rather than an outcome or a timeline, is what mounts us up with wings like eagles. When we fix the eyes of our soul on our Creator, we run without growing weary, walk without growing faint. This is training ground for our soul. When we make this shift, waiting no longer becomes necessary drudgery; it becomes a lifestyle of confident expectation in Him. Queue the *Rocky* theme song, please.

If our waiting season feels like sand slipping through an hourglass, what if we saw it as an opportunity to make the most out of every grain? What if we stopped living as a distant spectator to the ticking clock of our lives and allowed God to show us the meaning and joy in every tick and every tock?

Maybe that's what Vance Havner meant when he said, *"He who waits on God loses no time."*[ix]

When we aren't waiting on someone or something else to fulfill us, we can let God fulfill us right here, right now. When we stop dwelling on what we don't want out of life, we can start focusing on what we do want (and I don't mean that one thing outside of our control).

I decided to do one fun thing every single day. I took up gardening, even though I lack a green thumb. I started making my own sourdough bread, like Nanny. I turned dinnertime into dance parties and movie nights into galactic adventures with strobe lights. I jumped in the pool and played Watermelon ball with my kids. And in this process, I felt less co-dependent on my ideal outcome for my family. Deciding to enjoy my everyday life, at times, makes me forget I'm waiting for anything else.

Like Beth, I found my staying power. Staying power opened the door to acceptance, and acceptance opened the door to enjoyment. I still feel disappointment prick my heart occasionally, but I don't live there. It's not a period anymore; it's a comma. My story isn't finished yet, and more importantly, God is still finishing the work He started in me.

And here's one more *Rocky* quote for good measure.

"Going in one more round when you don't think you can. That's what makes all the difference in your life."[x]

A Prayer for Those Who Need Staying Power

Father, thank you for being with us in the fire. Thank you for using every season and every trial for good. Thank you that even when we feel confused, and our circumstances don't pan out the way we hope, we can hope in you. Lord, give me staying power. When I feel like I want to run back to what's comfortable and familiar, give me the strength to remain in your plan. Bring me supernatural peace, acceptance, and joy, even during a hard season. Help me to trust in your plan.

Continue praying in your own words …

Questions for Reflection:

1. Have you experienced others trying to rescue you out of your waiting season?
2. Which phase are you in, staying power, acceptance, or enjoyment?
3. What is the most difficult thing to accept about your current situation? What do you think God is saying about that?
4. What brings you pure, simple joy? How can you prioritize that more in your life?

Chapter Seven: Almosts

We recorded videos of our family and took pictures of our home to submit them to the country to request to be matched with two boys. Our agency found the brothers on a Special Home Finding list, a list of kids who are harder to place, such as special needs children, siblings, and older children. We felt relieved the country still agreed to work with us. We'd never been this far into the process before. It felt so close.

We paid for an adoption specialist to review the medical information. The doctor's assessment came back as expected. But we both agreed; we didn't see any reason not to move forward even though we didn't "just know" they were our boys. Who doesn't want that love-at-first-sight story? But we couldn't fake something that wasn't there. We were slowly coming to terms with our story looking (and feeling) different from other adoptive families.

At this point, we had waited four and a half years. Every year we discussed changing paths, and every year we naively assumed we were close to the finish line. *This year will be the year ... no point in changing directions... we've already paid ... we've already waited ... it's bound to happen soon!*

We felt optimistic about these brothers. *Maybe this is it!* We started talking about the boys by name, saying (not real names) "John could sleep here," or "you could share your Legos with Jackson." At the dinner table, we imagined their little faces, wondering what it would be like to have two more crazy boys running amok in our house. We welcomed the idea.

The holidays came and went, and our dream of sharing Christmas with all our kids faded. "Maybe next year" ... we grow tired of saying that.

We finally heard back from our agency. They selected another family for the boys. We were happy the boys found a forever home, but of course, we couldn't help but wonder, *when will it be our turn?*

Tragedy is not The Only Outcome

Cailey, and her husband, Chad, received their

first positive pregnancy before their 2nd anniversary. She didn't realize how much she wanted to be a mom until she saw that pink plus sign. Even though it was still early, they imagined what their life would be like in the coming months, discussing names and planning a special pregnancy announcement. They never imagined a painfully long visit to the emergency room and a traumatic miscarriage.

Cailey woke up the next morning wondering if it was all a nightmare, but the excruciating cramps quickly reminded her of reality. She furled into the fetal position, breathing deeply through every contraction. Returning to work a few days later, her co-workers (assuming she went on vacation) asked her, "How was your trip?" She forced a smile and swallowed her secret. A couple of weeks later, a friend posted a sonogram photo as a pregnancy announcement on Facebook; Cailey burst into tears at her computer.

Cailey didn't know anyone who experienced a miscarriage before. She assumed it was rare and was unaware of the risks of pregnancy loss, which made her feel more alone. She resorted to isolation and distraction, movies, television shows, anything to keep her mind off the pain.

The next time Cailey got pregnant, she realized seeing a "positive" test would always carry mixed emotions. She felt happy, but fear and emotional detachment crept in. After learning that first-trimester miscarriages are usually a one-time thing, she felt cautiously optimistic. Sadly, Cailey lost their second baby before she could schedule an ultrasound. Any healing she previously experienced was out the window. She cried herself to sleep many nights, assuming something was wrong with her.

Cailey's obstetrician poked and prodded, and the results showed a hereditary genetic mutation and a risk for blood clotting. At the time, little information was available for her diagnosis. The doctor sent her home with a folic acid prescription and told Cailey she'd likely have a successful pregnancy next time.

Chad and Cailey moved to San Diego the following year, and soon after found out they were pregnant a third time. The pregnancy made her feel nervous; it felt so fragile. Her heart couldn't possibly handle another loss. Up to this point, they kept their pregnancies a secret, even from most of their family. But they couldn't silently suffer anymore. They reached out for help and asked for church leaders to pray for a miracle. Each day they counted as a victory. But they lost that baby too. "Unexplained recurrent miscarriages" was the diagnosis Cailey received. She was distraught and felt inadequate and broken. Three months later, sitting in a fertility clinic, the specialist said, "you shouldn't be here at 23 years old." This statement reinforced the idea that there was something wrong with her body. The specialist offered a long list of invasive testing and talked about the possibility of considering IVF, but Cailey felt too overwhelmed to wrap her mind around fertility treatment.

Cailey no longer had immediate joyful reactions to positive pregnancy tests. Before her first loss, she enjoyed watching other people's pregnancy announcements. She would love to come up with a creative idea to surprise Chad, make it special, or capture the moment by video to cherish the wonderful memory. But she felt robbed of the ability to celebrate. Anxiety took the place of excitement. Cailey's fourth and fifth miscarriages both happened while she was leading worship services. It felt cruel, and it shook her faith to the core. With clenched fists and anger in her heart, she pleaded with God, asking Him, "Why do you even allow me to get pregnant if it's only going to be taken away every time?

Chad frequently asked his wife, "When was the last time you ate a meal?" There were many days she forgot to eat. She lacked the energy to do chores, walk the dog, get out of her pajamas, drink water, or even get out of bed.

Every pregnancy or birth announcement, baby shower invite, Mother's Day, or stranger holding a baby became a trigger, and she started to dislike herself for it. She hated hearing other women complain about their pregnancies. She would give anything to have morning sickness if it meant her baby was alive. Of course, she was happy for all her expectant friends, but she couldn't ignore the reminder of her failure to carry a pregnancy to term.

One day, Cailey's close friend pulled her aside at a women's conference. She listened to Cailey, cried with her, and allowed her to confide and confess every doubt and fear she held inside. Cailey knew this was God's reminder that even in all her brokenness, He had never left her. It was the first time she felt assured that God was not withholding from her or waiting for her to "do" the right thing. No matter how weak and vulnerable she felt, she could rest in the peace of knowing His grace is sufficient.

One year following Cailey's fifth miscarriage, she was in a better place. She could walk through the baby section in stores without a pit in her stomach. For the first time, she and Chad had intentional conversations surrounding the idea of "trying" to conceive (all their previous pregnancies were unplanned). They both accepted the idea that if they were to get pregnant again, it could likely result in loss. They were willing to take another risk. She began a regimen of supplements and made diet & lifestyle adjustments to prepare her body for conception. They removed expectations for a timeline. When they paid a visit to meet their new baby niece, they both got baby fever, and for the first time, they decided to "try" for a baby. They conceived immediately and tested positive within a couple of weeks. Though her heart was more expectant, she was still guarded and scared. She didn't want to get her hopes up but still wanted the baby more than anything.

Weeks passed, and Cailey conquered a huge milestone; she was already further along than all the other pregnancies. Her hopes began to rise. But one night, she experienced miscarriage symptoms. Chad relentlessly prayed for a miracle, but Cailey's jaded heart counted it as a loss. Her heart was too weary to persevere or ask God to save the pregnancy.

A week later, Cailey's follow-up ultrasound served as a déjà vu moment as she waited for the doctor to say, "your body already passed most of the fetal tissue." She knew what to expect; she'd heard it before. But this time, the doctor said, "there's the heartbeat." The doctor turned the screen, and Chad and Cailey saw their precious baby wiggling around, heart beating strong. Cailey spent an entire week mourning the loss; this felt like finding out she was pregnant all over again. The doctor checked for a rupture, but nothing could have caused the heavy cramping or bleeding. The only explanation was God's miracle at work.

The moment Cailey heard Evie's first cry, she breathed a sigh of relief. Her baby girl was alive; her heart was beating, and she was alive! In the weeks to come, she and her husband found themselves continually asking each other, "Is this real?" Cailey and Chad's love for baby Evie continues to grow more than they could ever imagine.

Although God healed places of pain, trauma resurfaced when Cailey had another miscarriage in March 2020. Her and her husband expressed gratitude for the privilege of Cailey's body housing another sweet angel baby, even for a short time. They decided to rest their minds on the promise of Heaven, finding comfort that their babies were loved and wouldn't ever have to endure the suffering of this world. The only thing they knew was Cailey's heartbeat and the presence of the Father in Heaven. And as they find themselves back in a season of waiting, they remember tragedy is not the only outcome.

Almosts

If you've walked through a long season of waiting, you are probably familiar with "almosts." Your boyfriend was *almost* the one. Your pregnancy *almost* went full term. The military *almost* sent your spouse home early. Your special needs child *almost* had a breakthrough. You *almost* went into remission.

Here's the thing about almosts: They feel good. After all, we've waited to feel something (besides discouragement) for so long. So, we hold on to the buzzing feeling of possibility, the hope that right around the corner, our "almost" could turn into a sure thing. We allow our minds to dream and our hearts to grow attached.

Although our story doesn't come close to Cailey's heartbreaking miscarriages, we have had a lot of "almosts" in this long journey to adopt. Almosts carry our heart sky-high when we hold tight to a specific outcome. If that outcome doesn't pan out, our heart drops from that sky-high place. After enough "almosts," we learn to protect our heart from skydiving because it wasn't made for that.

"Almosts" become a teacher, helping us discover the art of hoping ... teaching us to guard our hearts and put our hope in the right source. Hopefully, we won't build walls around our heart, but we will learn to guard it. Proverbs 4:23 tells us, *"Above all else, guard your heart, for it is the wellspring of life."*

It's not that we don't get excited or don't "get our hopes up," but we learn to proceed without tying our soul's worth to the outcome. We keep a restful anticipation, not an anxious anticipation. That's the goal anyway. I'm getting better at this, but I don't always get it right.

Hope is essential in the journey ... But where our hope resides is key. *"Now, Lord, what do I hope for? My hope remains in you."* Psalm 39:7

Yard by Yard

Every once in and while, my husband pulls his phone out and says, "you have to see this!" He played football throughout high school and college and knows a good play when he sees one. Usually, it's a replay of a killer touchdown--the perfect spiral landing in a player's hands. The player jumps over defenders, twists his body, and somehow makes it look easy to do gymnastics while catching a football in the end zone. Everyone loves a good replay. The world gawks at the mixture of athleticism and what almost appears to be luck. What we don't see in the replay is all the "downs" before that. The team usually reaches that highlight-reel moment little by little, yard by yard. Not to mention the endless hours of sweat, injuries, sore muscles, training, and conditioning it took to get to that particular moment in that specific game. We only see the thirty-second highlight. And this is what life feels like sometimes. We see other people's highlight reels; we hear the thirty-second summary of their story, their breakthrough. We see the picture on Instagram of their engagement ring, their book deal, their business endeavor, or their newborn. We don't see the yard by yard or the struggle behind-the-scenes. We don't see the wait. Sure, maybe they didn't have to wait long for the thing we've waited for, but nobody gets instant gratification in every area of life (and if they do, well, we know how that Hollywood story ends). While we might feel like we've only gained a yard in the past few years, someone else's perceived instant touchdown has the potential to bring major discouragement.

Bruce Feiler says, *"The smartest minds today — including those studying computers, biology, math, physics—have come to understand that the world no longer adheres to predictable, linear mandates. Instead, life is filled with chaos and complexity, periods of order and disorder, linearity and nonlinearity. In place of steady lines, observers now see loops, spirals wobbles, fractals, twists, tangles, and turnabouts."*

I sure relate to this quote, and I know friends like Cailey do too. If I'm honest, I expected more of a straight line out of life. I know it's naive, but it's hard not to slip into the "if I do x, God will do y" mentality. Our story looks less like a straight line and more like a tangled ball of yarn. I take comfort knowing that God can use ever loop, spiral and turnabout, all for our good and His glory—even my deepest moments of discouragement.

One More Time

In Mark, chapter 8:22-26, Jesus travels to Bethsaida and meets a blind man. He takes the blind man by the hand and leads him out of the village, away from the crowd. We aren't sure exactly why (maybe Jesus putting spit in his eyes is more of a private moment thing). After placing a spit and mud mixture on the man's eyes, Jesus asks the man if he sees anything. The man looks up and says, "I see men, but they look like trees, walking." Then Jesus laid his hands on his eyes again, and his sight was restored. For the first time in his life, the man saw everything clearly.

For a moment--we don't know how long exactly--the man "almost" has his sight, but not fully. I wonder how he felt during his "almost." Perhaps a mixture of excitement and fear, hope and possibility, a rush of emotions ... and maybe a slice of disappointment, wondering if the full miracle would ever come.

The blind man let Jesus touch him once more. Jesus didn't want the man to settle for blurry vision when He intends to bring him full clarity. What makes me pause and scratch my head is that the miracle didn't happen instantly; it didn't come without an "almost." Stories like this show us the heart of our Heavenly Father, who demonstrates that some breakthroughs come little by little, yard by yard.

What if we saw our "almost" as an opportunity for us to let Jesus touch us one more time? What if instead of pushing away our desires and Jesus because of fear of disappointment, we let Jesus come closer, trusting his timing and his process? He might need to pull us away from the crowds, and maybe the process is a bit messy and unconventional. Yeah, it's not a straight line -- that's not such a bad thing. God knows the straight line makes us flatline. The process of God pulling us away is an opportunity to experience a connection with Jesus that makes any glitzy highlight reel pale in comparison.

A Prayer for the Discouraged

Lord, I give you my feelings of discouragement. Even though I wish my path were a straight line, I trust that you use every winding and troubled road for your glory. Help me to trust you and to trust your timing and your plan. Help me to surrender the outcome to you and to allow you to change me from the inside out. Help me not to set my hope in the next outcome but in your unshakable character. Help me enjoy this journey with you, savor every moment, and find contentment in your arms.

Continue praying in your own words …

Questions for Reflection:

1. What "almosts" have you experienced through your waiting season?
2. How do you balance holding on to hope and guarding your heart?
3. How has your waiting seasons grown your character?
4. In what way do you need to trust Jesus one more time?

Chapter Eight: Holding Places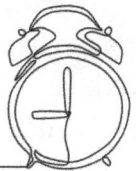

Many years ago, I'd pick up my youngest daughter, PJ, from the church nursery, and I'd find her in the same spot every time. While the other toddlers ran around the room smashing blocks and throwing foam toys, I'd discover PJ sitting next to her friend, Sienna, calmly snacking on goldfish or watching a video. (I'm not saying I have perfect children. PJ happened to be my one and only easy baby.) PJ has Disney bright blond hair with a fair complexion, and Sienna looks like a miniature Pocahontas. Their features, although different, complement one another, yin and yang. Even in diapers, they were kindred spirits. PJ and Sienna's sweet friendship paved the way for our families to become good friends.

Jenny (Sienna's mom) and I grew even closer as years passed, homeschooling our girls with the same curriculum and taking field trips together. Jenny and I share a special bond; we both grew up in broken families, Jesus changed our lives, and we work hard to create peaceful homes for our children and write a new family story. When our family moved away from California, there were tears on all sides. PJ and Sienna would be on opposite ends of the country, the yin and yang now bordering the Atlantic and the Pacific. We promised to be forever friends, no matter the distance.

Seven months after we moved to Florida, Jenny called me with a sadness in her voice. "There is something I need to tell you." Her voice trembled. "My marriage is over."

Jenny's whole world crumbled beneath her feet all at once, her heart fell into a sinkhole. Reconciliation wasn't an option this time; Jenny knew what she needed to do. But it all seemed too much, too fast. She needed to catch her breath and take time to recalibrate before filing for divorce. Jenny and the kids hopped on a flight to Florida to visit us in hopes of figuring out the next steps in their new reality.

Before Jenny arrived, I warned her about my new music selection and my attempt to brush up on my French. (Nearly all of what I learned in college is a distant memory, so "brushing up" is an overstatement.) I play French worship music while I cook and clean and play it while I take a bath. I listen to the songs to make a connection to the language, make it familiar. As soon as I turned on the first French worship song, I unexpectedly sensed God's presence on my skin like a feathery layer of comfort. Hearing God glorified in another language felt like seeing a diamond shimmer from a completely different angle. I am hooked. The songs ministered to me in my new, unfamiliar season, as I learned to relate to God differently, in a slower way. French worship reflects my season perfectly, learning to worship through the unknowns. I embrace the unknown lyrics the way I embrace the unknowns in my prayers.

My new playlist was the last thing on Jenny's mind as she faced her grief head-on. I created a plan for Jenny to help her find calm, clarity, and confidence during her stay. The plan included coaching, counseling, beach walks, working out, resting, good meals, and predictable rhythms. I called it her "healing retreat." We cried together a lot, went on prayer walks, and watched PJ and Sienna play with dolls at the beach. Brandon made us popcorn every night with his Whirly Pop machine, and we vegged out together, releasing the weight of our days with television and laughter and dark chocolate and popcorn (and dark chocolate with popcorn, try it!).

Jenny planned to move to Texas; the idea of temporarily going back to San Diego felt miserable. She'd need to go back, announce the divorce to the kids, meet with a mediator, and start sorting and separating all her belongings. She dreaded the very thought of it. "It feels like it's a temporary holding space," Jenny said.

Jenny slipped away for her counseling session. I turned on French worship music while she was out, wiping up the remnants of the morning's breakfast. An hour later, Jenny came back, dabbing tears from her eyes, telling me about her new perspective on her holding pattern. "God is the one holding me. God is holding us in his hands." She held out cupped hands, her eyes filled with a new revelation.

"During my counseling session today," Jenny said, using the edge of her tie-dyed shirt to wipe a tear from her eye. "I was sharing how much I dread going back to San Diego, how it feels like a temporary holding space. But then God spoke to my heart, 'It is a temporary holding space where I am the one holding you.'"

Jenny cupped her hands again, holding them out to me as a sign of her new truth. "God is holding me in his hands."

The worship music echoed while we spoke in the kitchen, an anthem of God's grace:

"Merci Jésus ..."

That line follows me around (Jesus is pronounced Jezu).

Merci Jésus in the shower.
Merci Jésus in the car.
Merci Jésus in my kitchen.
Merci Jésus on the beach.
Merci Jésus through all the unknowns.

Merci Jésus in the waiting season.

Merci Jésus in this holding space.

Merci Jésus, Merci Jésus, Merci Jésus.

Walking with Jenny through her painful season reminds me that a holding pattern can be an invitation for God to hold us. When we feel we have no other choice, nowhere to run, stuck in a time and space that requires us to hope and wait, it's an invitation to be held by our Father. His very name speaks of His mission: Immanuel, God with Us.

God doesn't always rescue us out of our holding patterns, even when they are painful. But He does promise to be with us, to stay faithful, to bring comfort, and to never leave us. There are times when the only position to take is the fetal position, arms wrapped around our Father's neck. *Merci Jésus. Even when I don't understand. Merci Jésus. Thank you that you're here.*

When our circumstances feel shaky and unreliable, anchoring our trust in the character of God gives us our steady footing. He is the same yesterday, today, and forever (Hebrews 13:8). With Him, there is no variation or shadow cast by turning (James 1:17). The unwavering love of God gives us something firm to grasp onto during times of uncertainty and prolonged waiting.

A Gift in Holding Patterns

This week my husband took our eldest daughter, Hannah, to California on a work trip. Hannah visited old friends, went ice skating, and attended her old youth group while Brandon worked. They were supposed to have a layover in Charlotte, North Carolina, before heading home on the flight back. But the flight from Charlotte to Palm Beach was canceled due to inclement weather. Collectively, we said, "this sucks" about twenty times while on the phone with one another. There weren't any other flights back home for another 24 hours. The airline paid for the next flight, but not for a hotel. They couldn't stay at the airport for 24 hours, waiting. We were all disappointed and ready to sleep next to one another again.

"Why don't you book a hotel there in Charlotte? Neither of you has ever been, make a day of it … a daddy-daughter day," I said.

Brandon took my idea and ran with it. After all, moping around the airport for 24 hours didn't sound like a brighter plan. They both slept in, went to brunch, spent the day at a science museum in town, and made sure to stop at the best Barbeque joint they could find. They sent me lots of messages, all bundled up and smiling in downtown Charlotte. They commented on how giant all the skyscrapers seemed after living in little Hobe Sound for eight months. When I finally pick them up from the airport, way past my bedtime, I asked them what their favorite part of the trip was. I expect to hear stories about our old stomping grounds, the San Diego weather, or our friends there. Instead, they both agreed the best part of their trip was the holding pattern in Charlotte. "I canceled work, I got to explore a new city and I got to be a tourist for a day. We had some great father-daughter time. It was the best part of the trip," Brandon said.

Holding patterns are frustrating and unexpected, but I wonder if God sees our holding patterns differently. Is He reaching out His hands to hold us? To offer us a gift? Is He extending an invitation to show us something beautiful? Perhaps God is smiling down at a daddy-daughter detour He has planned, but we keep dragging our feet, saying, "this sucks."

Andrew Murray says, *"The giver is more than the gift; God is more than the blessing. And our being kept waiting on Him is the only way for our learning to find our life and joy in Himself."*[xi]

When Brandon came back from that trip, I couldn't keep my hands off him. Of course, our kids couldn't either. Being away from each other wasn't a big deal when he worked 60+ hours a week. But with Brandon working from home now, I've grown used to having him around all day. I'm the opposite of a clingy person; in fact, clingy people repel me. But poor Brandon got a clingy version of his wife those first few days after he got home. I hugged his arm tightly, rested my head on his shoulder, kissed his cheeks, his lips, his neck, or whatever was within reach. He clung to me just the same, so I didn't feel so bad. We took the kids to the beach the next day, and Brandon and I laid on a blanket on the sand together. I let my body sink into him as he held me. We noticed the layers of blue starting from the water nearest us, all the way to the top of the sky. PJ built a sandman out of sand and shells, Bishop buries himself in the sand, and Hannah fell asleep. I could live in moments like this forever, holding and being held.

Most of my favorite moments in life include holding or being held:

The times I labored long and hard, rewarded by holding my newborn babies on my chest, skin to skin.

On July 24, 2004, when I stood before Brandon reciting our vows: "to have and to hold" ... and the minister pronounced us husband and wife, Brandon held my hand up high, like a boxing referee announcing a winner.

While throwing up during pregnancy, my husband held my hair.

Quiet mornings when my youngest snuck in bed with me, held my hand, curled up into my arms, and fell back asleep.

Hospitalized for croup as a child, my mother held my hand and stroked my forehead.

The time I babysat my sister, and she wanted to run away. I didn't know what to do, so I simply held her.

Watching my husband hold our newborn babies.

When I finally came to visit my grandparents after a couple of years in college, my grandpa greeted me with tears in his eyes, stretching out his arms; he held me so tight I thought he'd never let me go.

The time my dad held me after we received news of my mother's death.

Moments, where we hold and are held, are moments we cherish. They get seared into our hearts, tied to emotions, cataloged in our memories. God knows this, and He wants in on it.

The Psalmist David says to God in Psalm 73:23, *"Yet*

I am always with You; You hold my right hand."

In Isaiah 41:10, God says, *"Do not fear, for I am with you; do not be afraid, for I am your God. I will strengthen you; I will help you; I will hold on to you with My righteous right hand."*

David says again in Psalm 63:8, *"I follow close to you. Your right hand holds on to me."*

God reiterates His position in Isaiah 41:13, *"For I, Yahweh your God, hold your right hand and say to you: Do not fear, I will help you."*

Have you ever heard the phrase, "he's my right-hand man?" Many believe it came straight from the Bible because it meant a person held authority and honor; they were a trusted advisor, always at close hand. It was considered a rewarding place of proximity.

During seasons of waiting, let's not miss this invitation. God reaches out His right hand, offering to pull us in close. He is not a drill sergeant, commanding that we fall in line. He's a Father reaching out His hand to His child, saying, "let's do this together."

A holding place is not easy, but it doesn't

have to be lonely or purposeless. Let God be the one who holds you. Let Him pull you close. Don't waste a single day in dread or anxiousness. When you look back on this season of your life, I pray you look back and can say, "That was a holding place, a place where I was holding and being held."

When It Feels Like Wandering

I thought our adoption journey would feel like entering the promised land, but it turns out it feels more like wandering in the wilderness. That Biblical story perplexes me. Why did it take the Israelites 40 years to make a journey that should have lasted eleven days? Liberation from slavery in Egypt seemed like a step in the right direction, but after a while, they missed the familiarity and predictability of their old lives (Ex. 16, Num. 11). Maybe they got caught up in the "good old days" mentality and forgot the oppression of slavery. I don't know exactly, but I do know how it feels to want to retreat. When your future is unknown, it's hard to feel settled.

What does the promised land look like?
Is it just hearsay?

Is it really the land flowing with milk and honey?
Can we really trust God?

Ah, there it is. The question that it all boils down to. Can we really trust God? Can we trust there is a purpose in our wandering?

I've heard it was the Israelites complaining and disobedience that delayed the journey. But I think it goes deeper than that. I think God wanted to pull every last thread of slavery out of the hearts of His people. He wanted to secure their identity as sons and daughters. He wanted them fully prepared for their future.

We all read the Israelites story with an eager expectation for them to arrive at their destination finally; it's human nature. But intimacy can't be rushed. God wanted to reveal Himself in a new way, right there in the journey. We often become anxious for the mountaintop moments in life, but as one of my mentors, Greg Gorman, says, "There ain't no vegetation on the mountaintop. The valley is where you get fed."

The Israelites learned this the slow way, God providing manna for food, bringing water from rocks, parting the Red Sea, and leading them in a pillar of cloud by day and a pillar of fire by night. Baby step by baby step, the Israelites learned sonship through daily trust in God's provision. God wooed them into His arms, carrying them through the long journey, bringing them closer to a truth He wanted them to own: *My Father will take care of me.*

Holding places provide opportunities to be liberated from false mindsets around our identity. When we surrender to the process, we allow our Father to hold us and teach us to trust Him. Amid the wandering, He makes this promise, "My presence will go with you, and I will give you rest." (Ex. 33:14).

A Prayer for Those in A Holding Place

Dear Father, thank you for the gift of holding and being held. Thank you for the process of removing the lies surrounding my identity. Thank you that I am your child and dearly loved by you. Thank you for your good gifts, even gifts in holding patterns. Help me to step into full freedom and to trust you. Help me to understand the goodness of your character and your intentions towards me. Help me to rest in you and not in the outcome of my circumstances.

Continue praying in your own words ...

Questions for Reflection:

1. Do you see your waiting season as a holding place or a place where God holds you?

2. What are your favorite memories of holding or being held?

3. Why do you think the Israelites wandered for so many years in the wilderness?

4. In what ways can you prioritize your relationship with Jesus during your waiting season?

Chapter Nine: Expectations

Every Tuesday, my kids attend a culinary class at their homeschool co-op. I found this incredible co-op while I was getting my haircut last summer. We just moved to Hobe Sound, and I only knew two people. The woman getting her hair cut next to me asked where my kids went to school. I told her we were homeschoolers who just moved to the area and were looking for options for charters or co-ops. The woman was a walking billboard for a co-op nearby. She homeschooled her kids through high-school and raved about how this particular co-op set her kids up for success. She told me stories about the awards her kids won in college and went on about the teachers' passion. In short, she sold me. I signed up the same week. School dilemma solved.

The brilliant culinary teacher at the co-op shares a weekly lesson on different cooking styles.

All the kids cook together in teams. Their homework involves making meals at home, which I greatly benefit from. I started volunteering for culinary class and pretended to be a good-hearted helper, but selfishly, I wanted to learn to become a better cook. I met another mom who volunteered there also. Her name is Amy, and she's adopted multiple children locally. I told Amy about our journey and how we've waited for nearly five years. Amy looked me in my eyes and said to me with experienced conviction, "Your kids are out there, and the wait will be worth it. I promise you."

A couple of months later, I received a text from my new friend Amy. Amy said, "I just heard about a local sibling set, who are about to be adoptable. Are you interested?"

My heart dropped. The kids were in the age range we were looking for. Of course, I was interested.

Amy connected us with the child's guardian-ad-litem, which I learned is a volunteer advocate assigned to each child or sibling set in foster care. Their role is to stay connected to the child, spend time with them, and advocate for their best interest. They report to the social workers and the judge regarding what they believe is best for the child or children. The guardian-ad-litem's evaluation of the children's situation is greatly considered. All of this was new to me since I've become more familiar with international adoption than local.

We spoke with the GAL over the phone, gathering more information about the siblings. She served in the GAL role for the past five years, advocating for many different children. This was the first time she'd ever assessed that it was not in the children's best interest to be reunified. It was time to find these kids a permanent family.

We closed our international application entirely and decided to pursue this sibling set. It was a big step of faith. Opening ourselves up to finding our kids locally was an adjustment in our expectations, but we couldn't imagine traveling internationally during Covid anyway. Time for another detour.

Expectations

Many years ago, I hosted a women's group at my church. For years, every Saturday morning, we ate breakfast and drank coffee together while talking about God and life. The women's group bonded together with a group of ladies, unlike anything I'd ever seen. Many of us, though we live all over the map now, still keep in touch.

I met one of my good friends, Shayna, at our women's group. Week after week, Shayna shared the same prayer request - or at least the same struggle. Shayna was the kind of girl who *always* wanted to be married. As a little girl, she put on fake rings, pretended to be a bride, and wrote "Mrs." before her name. Shayna planned it all out; she'd be married by 23, birth her first child by age 25, and birth her second child by age 28. She felt confident her husband would be a tall, Southern man with blue eyes, brown hair, and a deep accent. But week after week, this man was nowhere to be found.

Shayna found herself 28 years old and still single. There's nothing wrong with that, but for Shayna, this did not fit into her timeline or her perfect plan involving her deepest desire. Throughout our women's group, the friends around her began getting engaged and then married. She attended weddings, became a bridesmaid multiple times, and hosted bridal showers for other ladies with an ache in her heart. Her happiness mixed with jealousy and disappointment.

Shayna tried the dating scene; the apps, the blind dates, the friend of a friend who was "perfect for her." She brought home men to her family, with trembling hands, knowing that it would probably not work out, just like the last time. Shayna was engaged once, almost twice. She had enough "almosts" to make her feel like someone tied her heart to a truck to drag it down a cement road. With every guy, she justified why it could work, why it could be a fit. Her desperation for a husband led her to compromise, making excuses for guys who didn't treat her with the respect she deserved.

One day, with tears in her eyes, Shayna took her list (the list of the timeline and what her husband would look like), and she tore it up. Her specific expectations made her feel like she was spinning in circles. Shayna was done with all of them. She was done trying so hard to write her own story, trying to contrive it all. She still felt like a part of her was missing; she still ached at the unfulfilled dream, but she was tired of the striving. She knew the desire to be married would never entirely go away, but she was committed to finding contentment without it. Shayna decided to stop dating for a while and took a break from even praying about it. She didn't want it to be the all-consuming focus of her life anymore.

Shayna and a guy named Wilson Kam both went to our church. Wilson was faithful and sweet, and Shayna had known Wilson since the 8th grade. Many people over the years nudged Shayna towards

Wilson, but Shayna always rolled her eyes. After all, he was just Wilson from the 8th grade. He's also Cambodian, so clearly, he was missing the blue eyes and Southern accent Shayna expected.

Wilson, in his own gentle way, pursued Shayna for ten years. Sometimes, he'd send flowers in secret on Valentine's Day. He invited her out to coffee or dinner, and Shayna would catch up with her old friend, oblivious to his feelings. Her time with Wilson always felt comfortable, like a favorite pair of jeans. But he was just Wilson from the 8th grade.

Wilson asked Shayna to dinner again, this time bringing her a copy of her favorite devotional. He found a copy with a pink cover, knowing pink was Shayna's favorite color. They talked and laughed as old friends do, and Shayna went home, thankful for her familiar friend, Wilson, from the 8th grade.

A few months pass, and Shayna decided to pray for her husband again. This time, it wouldn't be all-consuming, but she'd simply present her requests to God and leave them in His hands. Her devotional that morning spoke about the fruits of the Spirit, so she decided to say a prayer about that: *Lord, I pray that my husband would have the fruits of the Spirit in his life, that you would work these character traits out in his heart as you work them in mine.*

After her simple prayer, she hopped on Facebook. Wilson Kam updated his status just a few minutes ago. What was her friend up to? Wilson posted: *"I'm praying for the fruits of the spirit to be evident in my life today."*

Shayna sent me a screenshot and told me about her prayer. "Mel, this is creepy. How did this happen? I don't have feelings for Wilson. Does this mean anything? Am I crazy? How could Wilson post that right after I prayed for my husband?" I smiled, not wanting to sway her one way or another but sensing God was up to something special.

Shortly after Shayna prayed that prayer, she listened to a sermon. The preacher talked about how Jesus wasn't accepted in his hometown; therefore, he could do no miracles there. The pastor said, "Don't allow your miracle to become trapped in your familiarity." That statement punched Shayna in the gut. At this point, she knew she needed to give Wilson from the 8th grade a chance.

Wilson and Shayna started going on dates. But weeks went by, and she still didn't have feelings for him. He wasn't blue-eyed, he wasn't a Southern boy, and he didn't have an accent. And he was her friend--and *only* her friend--for 15 years. How do you take someone out of the friend-zone when they've sat there comfortably for 15 years?

Shayna realized that Wilson was everything she prayed for and wanted, besides her silly, superficial list. He was a man of character and integrity, a man who treated her with respect, a man who was thoughtful and kind and would make a good father. Even though he wasn't what she pictured for her husband, Wilson was handsome. Although she ripped up her list with her hands, this time, she needed to rip up her list in her heart.

Months went on, and Shayna was honest about her feelings, still uncertain. She'd flip-flop daily. This guy was great, but the feelings weren't what she expected them to be. Shouldn't she feel head-over-heels by this point? Shouldn't she be gushing and waiting by the phone? She kept going, not because she wanted to lead Wilson on, but because despite her lack of twitterpation, peace filled her heart when she was around him. She'd never felt that kind of peace in her past relationships, and she decided to pay attention to it.

One day, Wilson and Shayna went on a long walk together. Shayna's stomach hurt from laughing so hard. She realized two things on that walk: One, that she had never felt more like herself than she did at that moment with Wilson Kam. And two, a flip switched, she was not just attracted to Wilson, she was in love with him.

Not too long after, Shayna knew Wilson was not just Wilson from the 8th grade; he was Wilson, her husband, the man she'd waited for. Our women's group lined up as bridesmaids to witness Shayna and Wilson's union; we all thanked God for waterproof mascara while we dabbed our eyes through the entire ceremony. And one of the ladies from our group came up with the best hashtag for their wedding: #ItsAboutKamTime

Shayna's story is special to me for many reasons; one, because I witnessed her long journey of waiting come to a beautiful end, but two, because her story reminds me to hold my expectations loosely. Our expectations can become a roadblock to our breakthrough if we aren't careful. When we hold tightly to our ideas of how it will look, the timeline, or the way we will feel, we might miss the unique story God is trying to write for us. Shayna's story reminds me that just because my story is different from what I expected doesn't mean that God isn't in it.

Familiarity & Expectations

The religious leaders and most bystanders failed to recognize what was happening when Jesus died on the cross. They expected an earthly king, one to take over and change the political climate in favor of the Jews. When they saw Jesus dying on the cross, they missed the significance. They thought the hope for this political Messiah was over. But Jesus had much bigger plans than a local government takeover. His goal was to forgive sins for all mankind and provide full access to his presence at all times. I don't want to be like the religious people, wrapped up in my expectations, missing the miracle God performs right before me.

I wonder how many people bore witness to Jesus' death, who shrugged their shoulders and walked away. Perhaps some people thought, *just another criminal, just another day* ... Or *it's just Jesus from Nazareth, the carpenter's son.* While others pondered, *too bad, thought he would do something for the nation, but guess not.* I wonder if those same people made the connection to the Divine after he breathed his last breath and darkness covered the sky. Did they finally put the pieces together after water and blood came pouring from his side? After the earthquake, maybe? Or when word spread of His resurrection? We tremble at these stories over 2000 years later. We light candles and close our eyes, and we breathe these details in, imagining what it would be like to see the veil torn. We sing songs about these moments; we read the story, again and again. We use playdough and toothpicks to illustrate the significance to our kids in Sunday schools across the world. God's one and only Son sacrificed himself for us, with love too deep for our minds to comprehend. But some people saw Jesus with their own two eyes and still missed it. Their tightly held expectations of how God would save them, their familiarity with Jesus, and maybe even the fear of what others would think, all played a part in missing the most historically and spiritually significant moment of all time. I don't want to miss out on the fulfillment of God's plan because it differs from my expectations. What if our miracle comes in a different package than we expected? Will we miss it?

Peter Scazzero says it this way, *"Anytime we are clinging to or resisting something, we aren't surrendered."*[xii]

What are you clinging to? What are you resisting? Are you willing to surrender your expectations?

A Prayer for Those Surrendering Expectations

Dear Lord, thank you that your ways are higher than my ways and your thoughts are higher than my thoughts. Thank you for your plan, even if it looks different than my expectations. Help me to let go of any unrealistic expectations or expectations that differ from your plan. Help me to surrender those to you fully, to trust your plan every step of the way. When the plan starts to unfold, and takes a different turn, help me handle those changes with grace. Help me to trust you fully. I surrender. I choose restful anticipation.

Continue praying in your own words …

Questions for Reflection:

1. Do you struggle with holding on tightly to your expectations?
2. What expectations do you need to surrender to God?
3. What does surrendering to God mean to you?
4. Are you clinging to or resisting something?

Chapter Ten:
Unresolved Endings

I took writing courses in college and learned that you either end your story as a tragedy or a comedy, in other words, happy or sad. Um, I'll choose happy every time, thank you. I have a friend who loves tragedies. After watching a few of her movie recommendations, I started to see a pattern; this girl loved a good tragedy. *Ugh.* I proceeded to ignore her movie suggestions.

I pushed pause on this book for many months. Even though it was "complete," it didn't have the happy ending for which I hoped. I'm *still* in my waiting season. I kept thinking, *wouldn't that be nice if I could wrap the book up with a bow?* (Wouldn't it be nice if all of our waiting seasons held fairy tale endings?) The romantic in me wanted the happy-clappy, tear-jerking end to this book and to the story of completing my family. But life isn't seamless or predictable like Hallmark movies. It's full of ups, downs, plot twists, commas that we thought were periods, and periods that we thought were commas. We're left holding pieces of our story and wondering how they all fit together. I guess if you made it this far into the book, your waiting season isn't wrapped up with a bow yet either.

    Pursuing the local sibling set lasted an entire year, with weekly ups and downs. When one mountain moved, a new one appeared. The yo-yo became exhausting. But by the time Christmas of 2020 arrived, we were convinced the kids were ours. We couldn't imagine that God removed all those obstacles in vain. When placement didn't happen by Christmastime, we were given hope that maybe we could have a second Christmas with them a week or so after. The only presents left under the tree were the ones we bought and wrapped for the sibling set. We purchased a Magnatiles kit, Lego kit, and digital drawing board for the boy. We bought a bath bomb kit, a jewelry-making kit, and a sticker book for the girl. My friend sent an ornament with all seven of our names on it, and it said, "Together, we make a family." We had the kids' names embroidered on knit Christmas stockings to match all ours. I couldn't wait to see their faces when they saw stockings with their names on them. I know how much it meant to me when I needed a sense of family.

I held the kids' story close to my heart as I could relate to many aspects, including some of my deepest pains and insecurities. As I imagined passing that comfort along to the kids, it brought warmth to my soul to consider how God might bring that comfort full circle.

A week after Christmas, we were heavy-hearted when the request to transfer the kids to our home was denied because they were outside our county. This wasn't just another speed bump; this was a dead end.

I thought I was okay with it all. But I kept walking past the kid's presents under the tree each day, and every time it pricked my heart a little deeper. I felt sadder for the kids than I did for myself. I heard that the girl's only Christmas wish was to find a loving family. It didn't feel right that we held open arms forty-five minutes away. I asked if there was a way to give the Christmas gifts to someone to give to the kids, but they said no. They said foster kids rarely get to keep their belongings when they change homes, so it was pointless. But why did the adoptable kids need to keep changing foster homes when there was a forever home waiting for them? There wasn't anyone else in line to adopt them. The whole situation confused and disheartened us. I tucked their presents and stockings in a drawer where they remain today.

We waited in the international process for over four years and the local process another year. Here we are, over five years later, still waiting. This is not the ending to this book that I wanted (and certainly not the end to my story).

As I sat with a couple of friends for a fish-and-chips-style lunch, processing our journey and this book, my friend said, "Well, isn't there something beautiful about that?"

"About what?" I asked.

"A book about waiting, without a resolved ending. There is something beautiful about that."

These particular friends are the musical, beauty-is-in-everything types, and I guess I wasn't in the mood. *I bet they like tragedy movies too*, I thought to myself.

After sitting on it with God for a few weeks, I got back to my sweet spot of Restful Anticipation. I decided they were right. This book was never about my desired outcome; it was about turning my desire toward the one who holds my future. And collectively, as our world waits for life to return to normal after the pandemic, we all want rest amid an unresolved story. On a global scale, we wait for a resolution, for life to return to normal. But we aren't guaranteed when that will happen or what the new normal will look like.

Finding Restful Anticipation in the Lord is our only hope for turning our seeming tragedy into something beautiful. If we accept what is, not what should be, we find our happy ending on the inside. After all, that's what this book was about. God is up to something. He has good plans in store. I don't know what it will look like, but I anticipate something good, and my soul rests in that.

We may foster. We may raise money for a private adoption. We may give up on the idea of adoption all together (and support adoptive/foster families in other ways). We aren't sure yet.

As for now, I'm going to work on conquering that peanut butter jar.

Over the past five years, we hit speed bumps, roadblocks, detours, delays, and dead ends in our journey to adopt. How do you continue hoping after so much disappointment? How do you keep moving forward?

For me, I absorbed a truth that was hard-won — God is the defender and comforter of my heart and the upholder of my life.

"Behold, God is my helper; the Lord is the upholder of my life." Psalm 54:4

It's easy to fall prey to thinking others hold our future: our spouse, our kids, our boss, the economy, the government, our desires. But the truth is, God is the one who holds our future, and He is the one who holds our heart. He is the only one who can bring us grace and strength to meet all the unknowns that lay ahead.

If fellow waiting-people are anything like me, we've come to the place where we no longer want what we're waiting for to take center stage. It plays a part, but it's not the leading role anymore. For me, Jesus became the object of my affection, and I'm finding contentment living out my purpose in a different form.

The cry of my heart was to hang a stocking up for someone like Nanny did for me. I wanted to help a child find a sense of belonging and family. It might not look like what I thought it would, but I'm determined to live out my purpose no matter what. Lately, I look for ways to help encourage mothers, restore marriages, keep families intact, and bring wholeness to brokenness. Maybe I'll never see a new stocking hung in my home, but I'm committed to helping families ensure their stockings hang firmly in their own.

Often, we become so consumed with wishing our circumstances were different that we miss out on the opportunities to serve God right where we are. I want a heart that is willing to be faithful to God in all seasons, not just in the seasons I planned.

The *why* for my existence reaches far beyond my timelines, my expectations, and my unrealized desires. It is bigger than the size of my family or the nature of how my family grows. My purpose is bigger than what I get paid to do, what other people think about me, or my possessions.

As for my desire to kiss little toes once again? If that doesn't happen in the form of another child, you better believe I'm going to be the world's most eager Grandma. Maybe I'll go by "Nanny." Is it too soon to start planning that out?

You Know Who I Am

In John chapter 6, the disciples, surrounded by darkness and stormy waters, saw Jesus walking on top of the waves. The disciples panicked, but as Jesus walked toward them, he called out to them, "Don't be afraid. You know who I am." (TPT)

I know it feels dark. I know the waves seem choppy and uncertain. I know you are in the middle of the journey and don't know when you'll reach dry land again. I know how a season of seasickness feels.

But Jesus' words speak a powerful truth amid uncertainty: Don't be afraid. You know who I am.

These words feel like a call to remembrance, to remember who He has been, so we don't forget who He is today. I close my eyes and breathe in His soothing presence, whispering to my soul:

You know who I am.
I'm the one who heard your first trembling prayer.
I'm the one who showed you who you are.
I lifted you out of the pit.
You watched me perform miracles.
I stilled the storm to a whisper.
Have I not carried you through time and time again?
I am right here. I see your confusion and pain.
I held you before, and I'll hold you again.
You know who I am.

When I read that story, the red words, "You know who I am," jumped out at the page and into my heart. Have you ever had a moment like that? When suddenly, the words aren't just flat letters on a page, but they are personal. It's as if an angel got an assignment that day – a message from those ancient but living words—just for you.

I feel God speak those words to me almost daily now. When fear creeps in, I feel the Spirit whisper *You know who I am.* I'll be out on the patio, minding my thoughts, and those five little words wash up in my mind again like a message in a bottle. I'll be in the car daydreaming, and it's as if, for just a few seconds, everything else stops, and those words are the only thing that exist. *You know who I am.*

Many years ago, a pastor (who didn't know me) prayed over me and said, "There's something you've been praying specifically for your kids. I don't know if it's destiny or purpose. I don't know if you're praying for another child or contemplating adoption. I sense that it's like Hannah from the Bible, this desperation in prayer, this deep cry in your heart. But God wants you to know that He hears your prayers. He hears your prayers. You don't need to read all the books and know everything because you know God. It's simple: you know Him."

I didn't know what to make of that prayer when I first heard it. What does my desire for my children have to do with me knowing God? I didn't connect the dots. As I recall that prayer, all these years later, it becomes a fresh word. If *all* I receive out of my waiting season is to know God, that *all* is enough for me.

I am reminded of Jeremiah 9:24 (ESV), *"But let him who boasts boast in this, that he understands and knows me, that I am the LORD who practices steadfast love, justice, and righteousness in the earth. For in these things I delight, declares the LORD."*

I never really thought about my relationship with God like this until *You Know Who I Am* became personal to me. I suppose my relationship with God was more of a, *I sure hope I know Him*, rather than a confident *I know I know Him*. Those five little words are a love letter to me from God, an assurance that God will not waste my wait.

I grew closer to Jesus in these past five years. I don't hope I know Him; I know I know Him. And I wouldn't trade it for the world. This assurance makes me feel like Buddy in the movie *Elf* when his employer announces Santa's coming. Buddy jumps up and down with uncontrollable joy, exclaiming, "I KNOW HIM!"

The more I allow God to speak to me in the storm, the more I release my expectations. My formerly clenched fists turn upward. My heart surrenders and rests in His timing. I don't place my hope in a particular outcome; my hope is this: I know who He is.

> *"If the Lord Jehovah makes us wait, let us do so with our whole hearts; for blessed are all they that wait for Him. He is worth waiting for. The waiting itself is beneficial to us: it tries faith, exercises patience, trains submission, and endears the blessing when it comes. The Lord's people have always been a waiting people"*[xiii] ~ Charles Spurgeon

The Lord's people are waiting people, that's me, and that's you! He calls us His own and assigns purpose to our wait. I take comfort knowing there are more waiting people out there reading these words with their own unresolved endings. We may never meet face-to-face, but we share a determination to find beauty in our open-ended stories. I remind myself of King David's words in Psalm 27:14 *"Wait for the Lord, be strong and take heart and wait for the Lord."*

When we shift our focus, waiting no longer becomes necessary drudgery; it becomes a lifestyle of confident expectation in the Lord. No matter how many detours and delays you face, I pray you find your happy ending in Restful Anticipation.

A Prayer for Those with Unresolved Endings

God, I admit my story is not what I wanted or expected it to be. But I thank you for all the lessons you've taught me in my waiting season. You've grown my character. I'm not the same person that I was when I started. And even though this unresolved ending isn't what I anticipated, help me fix my eyes on you, the author and finisher of my faith. Don't waste my wait. Help me to know you like I've never known you before. Help me to find the beauty in this story, not the one I wish I had. Help me to live every moment in restful anticipation.

Continue praying in your own words …

Questions for Reflection

1. What are some different possibilities of happy endings to your story?

2. Is there anyone who inspires you with the way they navigate an unresolved ending in their life? What about them inspires you?

3. Do you hope you know God, or do you know that you know God?

4. What is the biggest lesson you've learned in your waiting season?

Epilogue

This book was complete and in the hands of my editor, but as I waited for the final edits, I received an unexpected phone call from the caseworkers of the local sibling set.

After the denial of the request to transfer the kids to our home, I forgot my husband wrote a letter. I had no fight left in me, but I supported his efforts. The letter (whom he sent to several prominent people in local politics and the foster system) explained our story, our desire to adopt the kids, and the roadblock we encountered. The letter begged for the decision-makers to remember why they took their job to begin with – to do what is best for the kids. He begged them to give our family a chance. After Brandon sent the letter, he heard back from one person saying they'd look into it, but we both surrendered and moved forward. It was all out of our hands.

Getting the phone call from the caseworker surprised me. Due to confidentiality, they couldn't share what changed exactly, but they said, "We are now considering your family to adopt these kids. It's time to set up a time to meet them." I've been shocked a lot over the last five years, but this takes the cake. I'm not sure what mountain God moved this time, but it must have been a big one.

A few weeks later, the caseworkers held a meeting with us, and everyone involved. The counselor will soon tell the kids about us and set up a time for us to meet them. To reiterate the seriousness of not giving the kids false hope, the counselor kept saying, "These kids have waited to be adopted for a long time. They've wanted it so badly." I wanted to tell the counselor, "We've waited to adopt for so long! We've wanted it so badly!"

I've been through enough ups and downs in this journey to know it's too early to celebrate. However, I sure am glad I kept those stockings.

To follow along with updates, join Mel's newsletter at MelissaMiller.Substack.com

Acknowledgments

Thank you to my husband; you have supported my love for writing from day one. You paid for every writer's conference, every coaching session, every book, and every program. You went on daddy-duty many times, so I could work on my passion projects and stay refreshed as a mom. You hold my dreams as if they are your own. I love you.

Thank you to Beth, Shayna and Wilson Kam, Cailey and Chad Brinkman, Jenny Garcia, and Scott Fay for trusting me with your stories. Your waiting seasons will not be wasted.

Thank you, Mom (Nanny), for being my safe place of shelter, my soft place to land. How different this whole story would be without you in my life!

Thank you to my mentors and writing coaches, Greg and Julie Gorman. This book would not exist without you. Your guidance is invaluable, but your character shines the brightest.

Thank you to my sweet editor, Maddie Buck. You are a gem to our family in more ways than one.

Thank you, Jesus, for showing me the beauty on the slow road. To know you and be known by you is my life's greatest treasure.

Endnotes

Chapter 1:

[i] Tozer, A.W. 1948. *The Pursuit of God*. Harrisburg: Christian Publications.

Chapter 2:

[ii] Elliot, Elizabeth. 1981. *Through Gates of Splendor*. Lincoln: Tyndale Momentum.

Chapter 3:

[iii] Buettner, Dan. 2015. *Blue Zones*. Washington D.C.: The National Geographic Society.

[iv] Spurgeon, Charles. 1859. "The Bed and it's Covering." *Sermon #244*. New Park Street Chapel, Southwark.

Chapter 5:

[v] Ortberg, John. 2008. "If You Want to Walk on Water, You've Got to Get Out of the Boat." Zondervan.

[vi] Michael Harter, S.J. 1193, 2005. *Hearts on Fire: Praying with Jesuits*. Chicago: Loyola Press.

Chapter 6:

[vii] Batterson, Mark. 2012. *Draw the Circle*. Grand Rapids: Zondervan.

viii 1976. *Rocky*. Directed by John G. Avildsen. Performed by Sylvester Stallone.

ix Havner, Vance. 2015. *Rest for the Weary*. Solid Christian Books.

x 1976. *Rocky*. Directed by John G. Avildsen. Performed by Sylvester Stallone.

Chapter 7:

xi Murray, Andrew. 1981. *Waiting on God*. New Kensington: Whitaker House.

Chapter 9:

xii Scazzero, Pete. 2020. *6 Radical Invitations from God for our Polarized, Politicized World: Part 1*. October 6. Accessed 2020. https://www.podbean.com/ea/dir-z2jvd-bb90388.

Chapter 10:

xiii —. 2015. *The Complete Works of C.H. Spurgeon, Volume 5*. Fort Collins: Delmarva Publications, Inc.

Cover image: Zoff/Shutterstock.com

Interior clock image: Singleline/Shutterstock.com